SHAKER

S H

JUNE SPRIGG and DAVID LARKIN

A K E R

LIFE, WORK, and ART

Photographs by Michael Freeman

A David Larkin Book

SMITHMARK

To S.E.L.

Published by special arrangement with
Stewart, Tabori & Chang, Inc.

This edition published in 2000 by SMITHMARK
Publishers, a division of U.S. Media Holdings, Inc.,
115 West 18th Street, New York, NY 10011.

SMITHMARK books are available for bulk purchase for
sales promotion and premium use. For details write or
call the manager of special sales, SMITHMARK
Publishers, 115 West 18th Street, New York, NY 10011.

Library of Congress Cataloging-in-Publication Data is
available.

ISBN 0–7651–1773–8

Printed in Japan

10 9 8 7 6 5 4 3 2 1

CONTENTS

A DAY IN THE LIFE

4:30 A.M. A late September Saturday begins, and it promises to be fair. The first bell rings. The Sister is awake already, but her eyes remain closed. She stretches in her narrow bed. The stove still sends out some warmth, but it will need to be fed, as usual. Her roommates are beginning to stir. Across the hall, and next door, the sounds of the Family waking come softly to the room.

She awaits her turn at the washstand and splashes water on her face. She pulls the brown and blue cotton-and-worsted gown on over her shift, smooths her hair under the starched white cap, and pins her kerchief across her bosom. The aroma of breakfast wafts up from the kitchen far below, but there is more than an hour until it's time to eat.

The Sister draws the covers back from her bed and folds them neatly over the foot to air the sheets and keep them fresh. She glides her broom over the smooth pine floorboards. The daily routine is familiar and comforting, she thinks, as she brushes some wood chips and ash from the floor near the stove. She wipes the woodwork—the window sill, the built-in drawers—with a cloth and brushes a small spider web from the shelf. She refills the lamp with oil from the big bottle, which is getting low, and reminds herself to ask the Deaconess for more. She moves quickly and is straightening a box of spools when the bell rings again. The quarter-hour has passed, and the Brethren are dressed and heading out to the barn to do their chores.

The Brethren gone, she steps across the hall and cleans their room. That accomplished, she returns to her room to sit and think about the day ahead while she starts work on mending the stockings that a Brother has left for her. She will begin a four-week shift in the kitchen this morning. It's been a while since her last turn there. This pleases her; she likes the activity and camaraderie. The holes darned, she picks up some kerchiefs to mark with her initials, tiny cross-stitches in fine blue thread. Her thoughts wander as the day brightens outside.

8

In the room across the hall, the Brother also hears the 4:30 bell, and he rises to dress and greet those who share his room. It's hard to get up today; his bones are feeling the years and the coming of the cold. The Sisters hung the wall cloths from the pegboard last week, and he's grateful for the extra bit of insulation they provide. He peers into the small looking-glass and shaves his whiskers off with his razor. It pleases him that tomorrow is Sunday, and he won't even have to do this small chore. He pulls on his cotton-and-worsted trousers, buttons his vest, and ties the laces of his boots.

He feels hungry this morning, but there's the milking to do before the Family can eat. He walks, slowly, down the stairs and into the bright cold dawn. The barn is welcoming and warm, sharp with the scent of hay. The sounds of crunching feed and the ring of milk in tin pails are a soothing daily refrain. He leans his cheek against the broad, warm, softly heaving side of the cow and feels the rhythm of the milking.

11

6:00 A.M. The breakfast bell rings. The Family moves down the hall to the stairs, exchanging nods and quiet greetings. Down the separate stairs, through the double doors, the Brethren and Sisters take their accustomed places at the tables, the Brethren on the east, the Sisters on the west. They are still enjoying the novelty of the new dining chairs, installed last month to replace the old, backless benches. These are much more convenient and comfortable, and deeply appreciated by all. After silent thanks, the Family sits. They eat without talking, murmuring only thanks for passing platters. There are, for this breakfast, boiled potatoes, fried sausage, wheat bread, stewed applesauce, and camomile tea. Coffee and tea were eliminated last year for the sake of health. The Family eats quickly, rises at the signal, and leaves for a morning's work.

The Brother gets his coat and hat and leaves for the Brethren's workshop, glad these days for its proximity. He stokes the wood stove and resumes his work on oval boxes. He has been making these boxes on and off for something like twenty-five years. In the summer, he continues to supervise the orchard work. Now, however, with the harvest in and the apples picked and stored, dried, or made into good, rich applesauce, he turns again to his winter work.

12

13

He begins today by cutting "swallowtails" into the strips of wood that
will form the boxes' sides. This is pleasant work; it busies his
hands, but leaves his mind free to drift. He remembers his first
efforts at making boxes—what an eager young man he was, full of
questions. Why were the swallowtails necessary? Why cut them with
a knife, not a saw? Why use maple for the sides but pine for the
bottom? He recalls the patience of the aged Brother who taught him
the answers that he, in turn, has passed on to young Brethren in
recent years. The swallowtails keep the joint from buckling by
leaving room for the wood to swell and shrink with time and changes
in weather from damp to dry. Cut them with a knife to give the
edges a slight bevel, rounding them so that the delicate points are
less likely to catch on something and break. Maple bends easily
when soaked or steamed in hot water, so it's good for the sides,
wrapped around an oval mold until dry. Pine is readily available and
easy to work—a nice wood for bottoms and lids. The Brother is
proud of his own contribution—using copper tacks instead of iron,
which rust and discolor the wood. The boxes he makes are as
perfect as anything on earth can be—an honest product of his faith.

14

The Sister is down in the kitchen. They will be baking today, and the fire in the large brick oven is already roaring. She and her partner will be making the pies this month, while others attend to plucking chickens and all the rest. They decide to take turns peeling and slicing the apples, planning thirty-five pies to last half the week. The work goes fast, and it's cheerful here. Soon it's time to clean up and set the table in the dining room upstairs.

11:50 A.M. The first bell rings. The Brother stands, stretches, and brushes small curls of wood from his work frock. He takes a quick count of the box sides he's finished—forty-eight. He steps back to the dwelling on the stone walk, while the rest of the Family converges. The dinner is delicious: chicken pudding, stewed onions, pickles, turnips, bread, and his favorite—apple pie.

4:30 P.M. The shadows are long. Now the Sisters' side of the dwelling is filling with light, and the Brethren's side is dim. The Sister yawns. Supper will be simple—just applesauce, bread, and milk. She misses coffee; her partner longs for tobacco, but that, too, has been discouraged. It has been a busy afternoon, preparing simple food for the Sabbath. Tomorrow, dinner will be baked beans and brown bread. The kitchen is spotless, ready for the day of rest.

The Brother is tired. He has soaked the forty-eight box sides, tacked them to shape around the molds, and set them aside to dry. If the weather stays dry and fair, they should be ready for lids and bottoms by Tuesday. He has spent the rest of the afternoon tidying and sweeping. He thinks back to his first days as a Shaker. It has always pleased him that his wife and children agreed to join, too. All have remained but his eldest son; it's such a long time ago since he left.

The bell rings again. He blows out the lamp, shuts the workshop door, and returns with other Brethren to the dwelling house. A single star gleams in the darkening sky. The dwelling house looks warm and inviting, bright with lamplight. All across the yard, Believers are heading for home.

A BRIEF HISTORY

THE SHAKERS, OR UNITED SOCIETY OF BELIEVERS
in the First and Second Appearance of Christ, were nineteenth-
century America's largest and best-known communal utopian society.
By 1840, nearly 6,000 celibate Brethren and Sisters lived and worked
in nineteen communities from Maine to Kentucky. The Shakers, or
Believers, were famous for their unusual way of life, for the
excellence and simplicity of their work, and for the dance worship
that gave them their name.

For more than 200 years, the Shakers have pursued their unique way
of life, based on principles of equality and communalism. Today,
fewer than a dozen Shakers remain, but the Shaker legacy lives on in
the creations they have left behind.

Shaker history in America began in 1774, when a thirty-eight-year-old
working-class Englishwoman named Ann Lee brought eight followers
to New York. Raised in the slums of Manchester, Ann, the daughter
of a blacksmith, was hardly a likely candidate for success. She was
poor, had no influential friends, and could not read or write. Yet,
while still a young woman, she possessed such powerful religious
convictions that she became acknowledged as the spiritual leader of a
small group of dissidents from the Anglican Church who came to be
known as the "Shaking Quakers" because of the way they trembled
when seized with the Holy Spirit. In spite of persecution and mob
violence, "Mother" Ann persisted in preaching.

In 1770, while she was in prison for having disrupted the Sabbath,
Ann had a vision that was to change her life and, ultimately, the lives
of thousands of others: it seemed to her that carnal relations were the
cause of most of the world's trouble. Her own four children had died
by the time she was thirty. Her mission was to teach a new way of life,
in which men and women were like children, as innocent in their
relations as brothers and sisters. Members of her new society would
live more like angels than like people, free from the age-old problems
of war, violence, greed, exploitation, lust, and every kind of human
abuse. Everyone would be equal, regardless of gender, race, or age.

Ann took Christ as her role model and taught that simplicity—material, temporal, and spiritual—was necessary for this new way of living.

Three years later, again in prison, Ann received a vision that God had a chosen people in America. The next spring, Mother Ann and her small group set sail for that bright new world. Among the faithful were her husband, Abraham Stanley, a blacksmith; her younger brother William Lee; and young, zealous James Whittaker, a distant relation.

Their arrival in New York was not auspicious. Lacking funds, the group separated and went to work to earn a living. Ann worked as a washerwoman; at times she was so poor that she had no food for supper. Things grew only worse. Her husband left her, impatient with her unswerving commitment to celibacy. Finally, in 1776, the group bought a small tract of land in Watervliet, near Albany, New York. Three years later, they built their first communal home. As if to mock their progress, the building caught fire and burned. Worst of all, they had attracted no converts in America after five difficult years. Somehow, Ann kept the others from losing heart completely, promising them that the day was near when eager listeners would "flock like doves to the windows."

Ann's prophecy came true the next spring, in 1780, when a religious revival swept through New York and New England. One of Ann's first listeners was a Baptist minister named Joseph Meacham, who questioned her closely on her unconventional views. Was she the "female Christ," as some were saying? She replied that she was not, but that as Adam and Eve were the "natural" parents of humanity, Christ and she were the spiritual parents of a new and higher order of humanity. With Christ gone from the earth, it was her work to bring word of this new and more perfect society. Convinced by her answer, Joseph became one of her first converts, and he persuaded most of his congregation to follow, too.

Fired by the growing enthusiasm of those who heard her, Mother Ann stepped up her traveling and preaching. But increasing interest in the new sect also brought persecution and imprisonment again; Ann was jailed from July through December 1780. In the following year, though, Ann embarked on a two-year proselytizing journey through Massachusetts and Connecticut. Missionaries had preceded her, attracting the attention of those who hoped to find salvation, as well as those who feared Ann as a British spy or witch. The trip was a mix of elevating spiritual success and humiliation at the hands of angry mobs in small towns. Exhausted, Ann returned to the home of Joseph Meacham in New Lebanon, New York, on the Massachusetts border. In September 1783, two days after a brutal attack, Ann returned to Watervliet. A year later, weakened by her experiences and saddened by the recent death of her beloved brother William, Ann Lee died at the age of forty-eight, after ten years in her "chosen land."

Mother Ann did not live to see the full flowering of Shakerism in organized communities, separate from non-Believers, whom the Shakers simply called "the World." At her death, those who called themselves Shakers lived in their own homes as individual families, maintaining their own farm properties but practicing celibacy and gathering to worship on Sundays. The creation of communal Families, who shared all their possessions in joint ownership and who shared work and reward as celibate Brethren and Sisters, was the contribution of Joseph Meacham and Lucy Wright, Ann's chosen successors. (James Whittaker died in 1787, less than three years after Ann. The loss of Ann was a severe blow to many who had converted because of her personal charisma, and James did not have the necessary temperament to guide the sect in new directions. Nevertheless, he kept most of the Believers together and in 1786 directed the building of a meetinghouse at New Lebanon.)

Ann's regard for Joseph, the Baptist minister originally from Connecticut, was high. She called him her "first-born son in America." She also thought very highly of Lucy, a bright young woman from western Massachusetts. "We must save Lucy," Ann said, "for it will be equal to saving a nation." Realizing that it was essential for the

Shakers to consolidate their material and spiritual strength to survive amid the temptations of the World, Father Joseph and Mother Lucy decided to set out on a new and unprecedented venture. Shakers were to leave their homes and live together in new communal settlements. Instead of rushing headlong into such an extraordinary move, however, they proceeded with great thoughtfulness. The society at New Lebanon, New York, would be the first to organize and would serve as a model in all things for other communities as they were established. Accordingly, in September 1787, Joseph and Lucy decreed that the time had come for the Shakers to separate from the World. About a hundred Believers were chosen to move to the adjoining farms of several members, bringing their possessions to be shared by all. A dwelling was built. The first meal shared by the new communal Family was Christmas dinner, 1787.

Father Joseph and Mother Lucy's contributions to the organization of Shaker communal life continued through the next decade. They established a system of "orders," or levels of commitment to the faith, to prevent hasty, impulsive conversions that would backfire in mutual disappointment. Joseph introduced a formal Covenant that all members would sign to declare their total spiritual and material commitment. In 1792, with the appointment of Elders and Eldresses to guide other newly formed communities, the "gospel order" of the Shaker faith was considered fully established. Pairs of Elders and Eldresses—bright, capable, and utterly devoted to the success of their unique experiment—went from New Lebanon to places where groups of converts who had worshipped together were now ready to take the bold step of living together. Across New England, Shaker communities officially "gathered into order"—Hancock, Massachusetts, in 1790; Harvard, Massachusetts, in 1791; Canterbury, New Hampshire, in 1792; Sabbathday Lake, Maine, in 1794—eleven settlements in all by 1794. Joseph also changed the way the Shakers worshipped, abandoning the whirling, shaking, and leaping of the first Shakers in favor of a simple, uniform dance that all Believers could practice as one, stepping forward and back in perfect unison.

Joseph died in 1796 at age fifty-four, leaving Lucy alone to guide the faith. It is a tribute to her skills and personality that she served as a second "mother" to the Shakers for the next twenty-five years, gently leading the group into its golden age of spiritual power. Heeding Mother Ann's prophecies that a second revival would take place in the West (present-day Kentucky and Ohio), Lucy sent three Brethren on a missionary tour beginning on New Year's Day, 1805. Their success was remarkable: nine new communities were established in the next two decades—five in Ohio, two in Kentucky, one in Indiana, and one in western New York State. The number of Shakers grew dramatically to about 2,500. Having survived internal and external challenges, the Shaker Society was a phenomenon unlike anything else in the New World or the Old.

Lucy died in 1821, leaving a society whose success would probably have surprised even Mother Ann. The next two decades witnessed further population growth to an estimated 4,000 to 6,000 by the 1840s, but no additional communities were successfully established. Significantly, the kinds of people who converted to Shakerism began to change. The original Believers, or "Mother Ann's first-born," had banded together to overcome severe local opposition and privation. Becoming a Shaker in the early years meant hardship, not ease. But as time passed, the Believers became increasingly prosperous, due to their simple living and thrift, and Shaker life became easier and more attractive to people of the World, including some who were more interested in a secure existence than in a soul-shaking spiritual experience.

The conflicts soon began to be felt. The Millennial Laws, first written in 1821, after Mother Lucy's death, were revised and expanded, codifying precisely what Believers ought to be and do. Some older or more deeply religious members felt that increased numbers were not necessarily a blessing, if converts came more for convenience than for a sincere desire for salvation. "Numbers are not the thing for us to glory in," they reminded each other.

By the mid-1840s, the Shaker population had already crested and begun its relentless downward drift. One by one, Families dwindled in size and ceased to exist. In 1862, a Brother from New Lebanon, visiting the Shakers in Union Village, Ohio, ruefully noted the decay of one Family's once-handsome brick dwelling, stripped of its woodwork and windows and open to sheep and hens, which lived as far upstairs as the attic. "Rather a costly hen roost & sheep fold," he lamented. In 1870, a Sister visiting a Family at Enfield, New Hampshire, sighed, "O how very few, only 10 Sisters and 9 Brethren; but O how we pray that there might be a gathering in this place." Those prayers were not answered. In 1875, at Tyringham, Massachusetts, the first entire community closed.

Today, fewer than a dozen Shakers remain in America, in two of the original nineteen communities: Canterbury, New Hampshire, and Sabbathday Lake, Maine. The oldest Shakers, who are in their eighties and nineties, have witnessed the near-extinction of their way of life. All but the first closings of the other communities have occurred within their lifetime.

How do the Shakers feel about the future of their way of life? Eldress Bertha Lindsay, who has spent more than eighty years at Canterbury, where she came as a little girl, recalls with sadness the 1965 decision to close the Covenant and cease taking in new members. She says, "We don't want to close our doors. I would like the churches all to fill right up with Shakers again."

She believes that whatever happens, however, the spirit of the Shakers will never truly die. She points to a renaissance of interest in the Shakers with pride and pleasure, sharing the admiration for those whom she reverently calls the "old Shakers." Bertha also views with enthusiasm the restoration of Shaker villages and the interpretation of Shaker life and work in museums. While there are no longer Shakers at most of the places mentioned and shown in this book, she enjoys hearing of the successful new careers of the former Shaker communities as museum villages. At Hancock, Massachusetts, and the two Shakertowns at Pleasant Hill and South Union, Kentucky, visitors can see restored buildings and Shaker furnishings in their original settings. At the Fruitlands Museums in Harvard, Massachusetts, and the Shaker Museum in Old Chatham, New York, those who appreciate Shaker design can tour fine collections in museum settings. At Sabbathday Lake, visitors can tour Shaker buildings and have the opportunity to meet and talk with surviving Believers. They can do the same at Canterbury, where a museum organization called Shaker Village, Inc., was created in 1974 to help the Shaker Sisters preserve the village for the future as a restoration, and as their home now.

Sister Frances Carr of Sabbathday Lake, a generation younger than Eldress Bertha, hopes that the Society will not come to an end. She points to the presence of three dedicated young newcomers to her community who are seeking to continue Shakerism as the "old Shakers" knew it, with large communal Families and many hands to share the work and blessings. Although the three have not signed the Covenant, they are accepted as Believers in their community.

Mother Ann herself foretold the rise and fall of the brave new world she envisioned, and predicted that when there were as many Shakers left as there are fingers on a child's hand, there would come another revival and a second flowering of the faith. The day is perhaps not far distant when only five Shakers will remain. The Believers and the World can only wait and see what happens. Meanwhile, as Eldress Bertha says, "The hands drop off, but the work goes on."

Few material traces of Mother Ann Lee exist, and no words were ever written by her—she could neither read nor write, as was typical of working-class women in America and Britain in the eighteenth century. However, a few remaining objects were prized by the Shakers as having been associated with Mother Ann. This rocking chair (with rockers added later to an old New England Windsor chair) was treasured by the Shakers at Harvard, Massachusetts, as "Mother Ann's chair." Ann Lee's ties with the Harvard community were special. She lived at Harvard for two years, 1781 to 1783, during her prolonged missionary tour of New England. Here, she said that she found God's "chosen people in America," whom she had seen in a vision before her departure from England.

The Meetinghouse at Sabbathday Lake, Maine, remains virtually unchanged since its construction in 1794; its details have been preserved in pristine condition. The building's timber frame was raised on June 14, 1794, under the direction of Moses Johnson (1752–1842), the master builder sent from New Lebanon, New York, to ensure that the Shaker meetinghouses conformed to the New Lebanon prototype. Like all of Moses Johnson's meetinghouses, the building has a gambrel roof and separate doors for Brethren, on the left, and Sisters, right. The 20,000 bricks required for the two chimneys were made by Brother Ephraim Briggs, who completed all the carpentry work.

The Meetinghouse at Canterbury, New Hampshire, was framed by
Moses Johnson (1752–1842) in 1792 as a replica of the 1786
Meetinghouse at New Lebanon, New York. This view, from the
belfry of the Church Family Dwelling, shows the distinctive gambrel
roof and the stairwell at the rear, with steep steps leading up to the
Ministry's quarters on the two upper floors. The rooms on the near
side were occupied by Job Bishop (1760–1831), one of Mother Ann's
best-regarded young followers, who was sent by the New Lebanon
community to head the New Hampshire Ministry in 1792. His
"proverbial piety, accomplished manners, and sound sense" did
much to guide the community's growth.

Ann Lee died in 1784, after ten years in America, exhausted by
physical persecution by mobs and saddened by the death six weeks
earlier of her beloved younger brother William. Mother Ann was
laid to rest at Watervliet, New York, her first and last Shaker home
in the New World.

In 1805, Mother Lucy Wright sent three Shaker Brethren as missionaries to the American West, then in Ohio and Kentucky. The three walked more than 1,000 miles after starting on foot from New Lebanon, New York, at 3 A.M. on New Year's Day. One, "Little Benjamin" Youngs, weighed only 100 pounds, but all three proved indomitable. By 1815, six new communities had been established in the West, with two more to come. The success of the western mission gave new hope and energy to Believers everywhere.

Pleasant Hill, in the bluegrass region near Lexington, Kentucky, was one of the new societies. Like all the others, this community followed the lead of New Lebanon in all matters. Shaker furniture, architecture, dress, and song were remarkably alike in villages as far apart as Maine and Kentucky. Here, the Center Family Dwelling at Pleasant Hill is visible in the distance.

Shaker villages were characterized by neatness and extreme simplicity. Architecture was unadorned. "Beadings, mouldings and cornices, which are *merely for fancy* may not be made by Believers," reminded the Millennial Laws of 1845. "Odd or fanciful styles of architecture" were likewise prohibited. The Laws also prescribed paint colors suitable for buildings in various parts of the village. Wooden buildings along the street were to be "of a lightish hue"; barns and other back houses, of a darker hue, such as red, brown, or "lead color." The Meetinghouse alone was white.

Here, two small outbuildings at Pleasant Hill, Kentucky, reflect the instructions of the Millennial Laws. On the left is the Water House, which contains a 17,600-gallon cistern for spring water, pumped in by horsepower. The cistern was begun in 1831, and the building was completed in 1833. To the right is the Bath House for the Brethren of the Center Family, built in 1860; a similar structure for the Sisters no longer stands. Personal cleanliness was as important to the Shakers as order in their dwellings and shops.

Eldress Gertrude Soule knits a baby bonnet for a worldly friend on the porch of the Dwelling House at Canterbury, New Hampshire. She joined the Shakers in Maine as a young girl with her sister. Today, she greets visitors to the Shaker village daily when the buildings are open to the public in summer and fall. Eldress Gertrude's warmth and humor surprise many visitors, who expect the Shakers to be a solemn lot. (Recognizing that her society has shrunk to fewer than a dozen members in America, Eldress Gertrude sometimes refers to the Shakers as "an endangered species.") Now in her nineties, Eldress Gertrude continues to wear traditional Shaker dress—a calf-length pleated dress with a shoulder cape, or "bertha," and a starched white net cap, symbol of the Sisters' celibate purity.

34

Unlike the Amish, with whom they are sometimes compared, the Shakers were always amenable to accepting technological progress, including electricity, indoor plumbing, telephones, televisions, and automobiles. In 1918, a group of Shaker Sisters from Canterbury, New Hampshire, clearly enjoyed their apple-picking outing in early fall. The two Sisters in the back row nearest the truck's cab still live at Canterbury. Eldress Bertha Lindsay, on the right, is the community's leader; Sister Ethel Hudson, on her right, still occupies the village's large communal Dwelling.

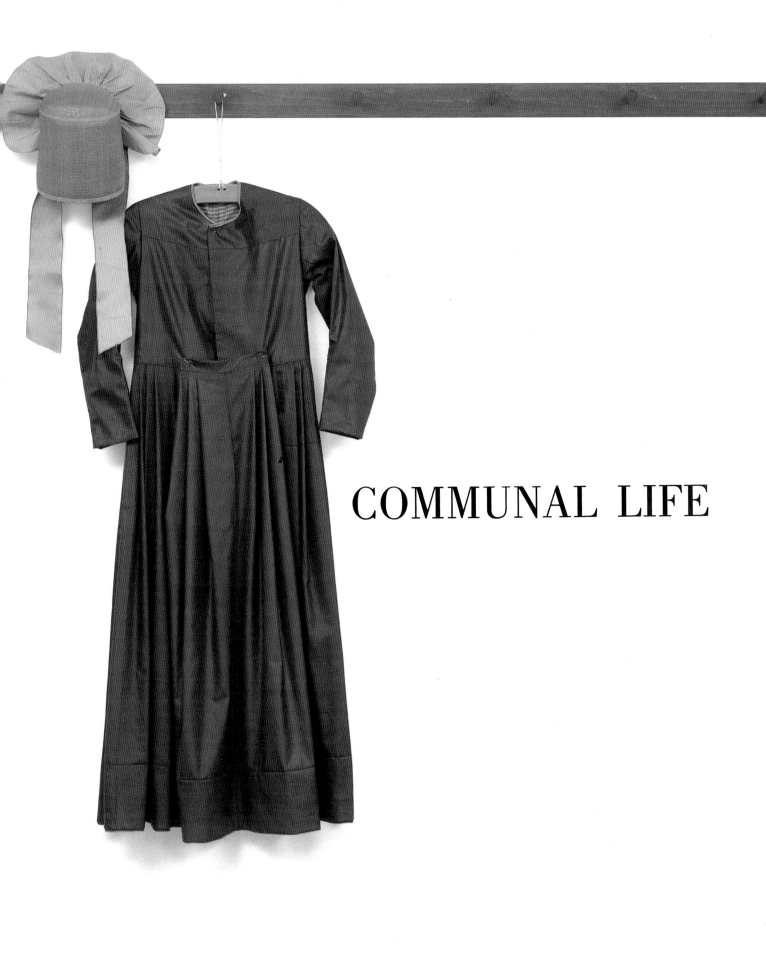

COMMUNAL LIFE

THE SHAKER EXPERIMENT IN COMMUNAL LIFE

formally began in 1787, when Father Joseph Meacham and Mother Lucy Wright gathered a hundred Believers to live and work together in a community at New Lebanon, New York. It was a bold and innovative step. While many attempts at communal life were tried in the mid-nineteenth century—Ralph Waldo Emerson exclaimed in 1840 that Americans were "all a little wild here with numberless projects of social reform—not a reading man but has a draft of a new community in his waistcoat pocket"—the Shakers in 1787 had no model to copy. The Yankee farmers and tradespeople who composed the first generation of Believers were not familiar with earlier ventures in communalism, at the Ephrata Cloisters in Pennsylvania, or at the semicommunal Moravian settlements in Pennsylvania and farther south. Nor were the Shakers familiar with the monastic traditions of Catholic Europe. Joseph and Lucy were starting fresh, and their organizational abilities were instrumental in the Shakers' success. By 1794—twenty years after Mother Ann Lee's arrival in New York—there were eleven established Shaker villages in New York and New England.

Life was not easy in the first years. The areas where the Shakers had settled did not necessarily have the best farmland in the Northeast, although the Believers in each community gathered on the best land available to them. In New Lebanon, Shakers assembled at the home

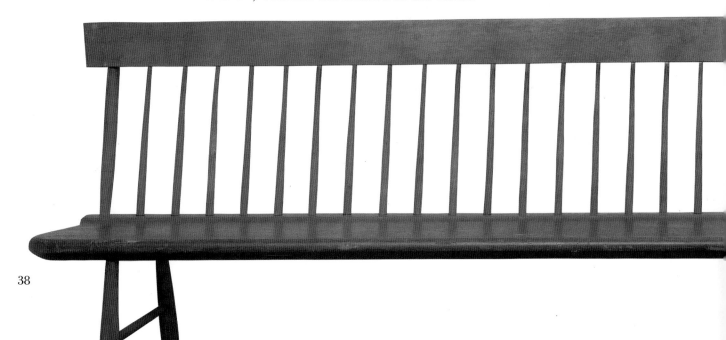

of George Darrow, in the hills along the Massachusetts border. At Canterbury, New Hampshire, the first Believers came to the farm of Benjamin and Mary Whitcher in the granite hills twelve miles north of Concord. At Sabbathday Lake, Maine, the Believers moved to Gowen Wilson's farm. It was difficult to make single-family farms produce enough food for dozens of new members. Shakers everywhere spent the first years improving fields and crops, erecting dwellings big enough to accommodate large Families, and building workshops where they could manufacture goods for their own use and for sale to supplement their income.

Calvin Green described his experience at New Lebanon in 1788, a drought year, when he was only eight. "We had very little bread," he recalled years later, "not much milk, scarcely any pie, butter or cheese. We had to live on meat, such fish as we could get, porridge, salt meat, broth and potatoes. For a time potatoes were our chief food. . . . [We] worked hard and were not overfed. I was hungry all the time." Similarly, Rebecca Clark remembered her first year at Hancock, Massachusetts, in 1791, when she was twenty-one:

> There were nearly a hundred in the Family where I lived. . . . Fourteen of us slept in one room. . . . Our buildings were small and we had to eat and live accordingly. . . . Our beds, bedding, and clothing that we brought with us, we all divided among the

members of the Family, as equally as we could. . . . We were all much engaged to build buildings, and to raise provisions, and gather a substance to live on. Our food was very scanty, but what we had we ate with thankful hearts.

At Canterbury, New Hampshire, the conversion to communalism took place with relative ease, as Benjamin and Mary Whitcher had already "most generously and conscientiously opened their doors and spread their tables in welcome to everyone who came to seek for the truth." Forty-three people were living at the Whitchers' farm when the community was formally recognized by the New Lebanon society in 1792.

To help all the communities succeed, Father Joseph and Mother Lucy decided that a hierarchy was needed, a system of "orders," or different communal Families, geared to the special needs and abilities of different kinds of converts. The original society at New Lebanon consisted of three orders. The first order included young unmarried people who were primarily indoor workers—that is, artisans and craftspeople. The second order was composed of young unmarried Believers whose work was principally outdoors—farmers, woodcutters, shepherds, and the like. The third order consisted of older converts, including those who had been married, and business-oriented people, like shopkeepers and those with skills in commerce and real estate. In 1799, Mother Lucy established two additional orders—a children's order, where youngsters not yet in their mid-teens lived with supervisors known as caretakers; and a novitiate, or "gathering," order, where people attracted to the Shaker way of life could see if it was something that they really wanted. Newcomers to the faith were known as "young Believers," no matter how old they were. The system was sufficiently flexible to evolve with the changing needs of the sect. By the early nineteenth century, the standard hierarchy in a Shaker community consisted of three distinct orders based loosely on the original plan, but with more formal legal arrangements between converts and the society. If the prospective convert and the leaders agreed that advancement was desirable, the next step after the novitiate was a junior order, whose members freely gave their labor to the community but retained their own property. The final step was the senior order, whose members signed the Covenant to declare their full spiritual and material commitment to the society. Senior-order Shakers freely gave their services, relinquished their property to communal ownership, and fully intended to remain with the Shakers for the rest of their lives.

By 1825, the Family, or order, structure had taken its final shape. Most communities had at least three Families. New Lebanon, the largest eastern community, had eight. The oldest, central, and largest Family in each community was called the Church Family (the Center Family in Kentucky). The Church Family, a senior order, was the site of the single Meetinghouse that the entire community shared. Other Families in each community were named for their geographical relationship to the Church Family—East, West, North, South—or occasionally for another identifying feature, such as Hill or Brickyard. Each Family had its own dwelling, barns, workshops, and enterprises. Members were not encouraged to visit other Families without a specific reason or without permission. The term "Family" in Shaker use meant a place as well as a group of people. In this sense, Families, usually a quarter- to a half-mile apart, were like neighborhoods.

New Families were established as the communities grew. At Hancock, for example, the Church Family gathered in 1790. In 1792, it was joined by the West and Second Families, both junior orders, and the East Family, a novitiate order. In 1800, the South Family was added as a second novitiate order. In 1822, the North Family, a senior order established to accommodate the overflow from the Church Family, was the sixth and final Family to incorporate as part of the Hancock community.

In addition to the system of orders and Families, Joseph Meacham and Lucy Wright instituted a system of leadership. Each Family had three sets of leaders: a pair of Elders and a pair of Eldresses (one of each pair was an assistant or junior member), who were in charge of their Family's spiritual well-being and of things in general; two Deacons and two Deaconesses, who were authorized to handle all practical concerns—such as laundry, meals, and the farm work schedule—and to provide tools, furnishings, and clothing as requested by the Family; and four Trustees, two of each sex, who lived in the Family's business office and were responsible for the Family's financial success and for transactions with the World. The Elders and Eldresses of the Church Family were also responsible for the entire community in general.

In turn, the Church Family Elders and Eldresses in each community were answerable to a higher authority, the two Elders and two Eldresses of the Ministry. Just as each Family was part of a larger community, so each community was part of a larger unit known as a bishopric. The Maine Bishopric had two communities, at Sabbathday Lake and Alfred. The New Hampshire Bishopric also had two communities, at Canterbury and Enfield. The Hancock Bishopric included Hancock and Tyringham, in western Massachusetts, as well as Enfield, Connecticut. It was the job of each bishopric's Ministry to oversee the spiritual and organizational well-being of each community in its care. The Ministry divided its time equally among its communities and spent considerable time traveling. It also kept closely in touch with the society at New Lebanon, the model for all other communities.

The final and highest authority in Shaker leadership was the Ministry at New Lebanon, which was regarded as the "capital" of the Shaker world. Bishopric Ministries were answerable to the Parent Ministry at New Lebanon, whose authority was revered because it descended in a direct line from Mother Ann. Ann chose Father Joseph and Mother Lucy as her successors. Lucy selected Ebenezer Bishop and Ruth Landon as her successors. In turn, Ebenezer and Ruth chose their successors, and so on through the years. It was customary for the junior partner to succeed the senior partner in the Ministry and Elders' positions, although circumstances sometimes dictated otherwise. The system was not perfect, but it generally worked well, with natural leaders rising to authority by virtue of their industry, charity, honesty, and common sense. It was usually the consensus of the Family that those who served as its leaders had been rightfully chosen.

With the communal framework solidly in place, the Shakers began to face the special circumstances of living a communal *and* celibate life—a combination so unusual that most worldly observers could scarcely comprehend it. "Their vow is celibacy; and they have everything in common," a Scottish visitor observed in 1841. "How they manage with their combs and tooth-brushes, I did not presume to ask them." Nathaniel Hawthorne decried the lack of privacy. Charles Dickens sniffed that rumors of secret romances were unlikely if all Shaker women were as unattractive as the one he had met. Serenely oblivious to the World's opinion, however, the Shakers set about solving problems with good sense, charity, and the ability to forgive.

One of the keys to success was order in every part of life. It simply worked best for the Family to do things according to a set schedule— to rise at the same time, to gather for meals at fixed hours, to begin and end work and retire for the night at the same times. Accordingly, the Shakers adapted their individual "time clocks" to the needs of the Family. Believers rose with the bell at 4:30 A.M. in summer, knelt in prayer, and pulled back the covers to air the beds. (The hour of rising in winter was 5:30 A.M.) In fifteen minutes, they were dressed and out of their "retiring rooms." Breakfast was an hour and a half after rising, dinner was at noon, and supper was at 6 P.M.

Believers entered the dining room in an orderly fashion. "Ye shall have no talking, laughing, sneering, winking, blinking, hanging and lounging on the railings, hugging, fumbling, and fawning over each other, when going to the table," reminded the Holy Orders of 1841. "And there shall no whispering, laughing, sneering or blinking be done or carried on at the table." Believers knelt together in silent prayer and dined in silence—an understandable rule to anyone who has heard the racket of a hundred voices in a wood and plaster room.

There were Family meetings every week night except Monday, which was an evening off. Meetings began at 7:30 P.M. in summer (a half-hour later in winter) and were preceded by "retiring time," a quiet period with no unnecessary talking or movement. After meeting, the Family retired for the night. The occupants of a "retiring room" were required to go to bed at the same time, unless prevented by necessary chores. Brethren and Sisters were not allowed to "sit up after the usual time of retiring to rest, to work, read, write, or any thing of the kind," without the permission of the Elder or Eldress. Such a regulation prevented individuals from exercising too much self-interest, and also helped reduce the risk of fire from candles or lamps. The Millennial Laws of 1845 prohibited the carrying of lamps or candles if they were not safely enclosed in a lantern, and also forbade smoking and working at the same time.

Order was also important in the physical environment. To avoid chaos in the dwelling and workshops, furnishings and tools were often marked to indicate their proper location; Mother Ann had advised her followers to keep things in such order that they could be found, day or night. Consideration was also essential in daily life. Believers were taught to speak and move quietly. "You ought to pass each other like angels," Father William Lee had said. During the Civil War, a toughened Texas Ranger could not believe that ninety people shared one dwelling at South Union, Kentucky. "If so many of us lived in one house," he declared, "we should fight and kill each other." Weekly confession to the Elder or Eldress helped to clear the air and maintain good feelings.

Uniformity was another key to success. No member was to have things better than the rest. Furnishings were kept to a minimum for the sake of simplicity and order. "Retiring rooms" were typically furnished with a chair and a narrow bed for each occupant, a wood-burning stove, a strip of carpet, a washstand, looking-glass, and towels, a few brooms and brushes, and little else.

Celibacy also required certain rules. The Shakers were distinctive among celibate sects for not cloistering men and women in separate dwellings. Instead, Brethren and Sisters had separate quarters in the same Family dwelling. It was "contrary to order" for individuals of the opposite sex to develop special, private relationships, lest they fall into temptation. Father Joseph realized early on, however, that friendship between the Brethren and Sisters was a good thing, given proper supervision. To this end, he established popular evening "union meetings," in which small groups of Believers met and visited informally or sang. There were three union meetings a week. Members of the groups were occasionally rotated to foster wider friendships and to minimize the chance of budding romance.

Boys and girls were more strictly segregated than were the adults. There were separate girls' and boys' houses, with two caretakers of the appropriate gender for each group. Although boys and girls received the same kind of education, they attended school at different times of the year—girls in summer, when the boys were needed for farm work, and boys in winter, for terms of about three months each. Children who were raised by the Shakers either came with their parents or were taken in as charitable wards from broken homes. As well as book learning, Shaker children learned trades in an apprenticeship system similar to that of the World. Although the young people raised by the Shakers were not required to sign the Covenant and stay when they turned twenty-one, older Believers naturally hoped that they would remain and perpetuate the community's labor and values. Sadly for the Shakers, many of the young people were either forcibly removed by their families or left on their own to explore the beckoning World.

Not everyone who tried the Shaker life found it suited to his or her needs, and not everyone who wanted to become a Shaker could make the requisite sacrifices easily. Shaker journals are scattered with references to the departure of Believers. Those who chose to leave in a forthright manner were treated with charity, although regarded with disappointment. In 1833, Peter Peterson honorably announced his decision to leave. He received clothing, a gift of $40, and a ride to the stagecoach to Albany, where his fare was paid. A Brother even assisted him with his trunks. But the more usual way to leave was to sneak off. Believers who left that way were often *not* sorely missed, as they were likely to have had problems adjusting to Shaker life in the first place. In 1816, a Believer noted, "Rebecca Quicksels goes off— good riddance." Believers who couldn't make up their minds whether to go or to stay were sometimes taken back for another try, sometimes with success and sometimes not. In 1836, Silvanus Rice of New Lebanon, New York, went "to the World"—again. "This is his second trip," a Brother wrote, "& I reckon he has learned the road to perdition well by this time." Opportunistic converts were known as "winter Shakers" (for the season when work was lighter) or as "bread-and-butter Shakers."

Although it is commonly assumed that celibacy doomed the Shakers to eventual decline, that is not necessarily true. Celibacy eliminated the guaranteed replacement of numbers through children, but it also meant that the people who lived in Shaker villages *wanted* to be there and had voluntarily chosen to make the necessary sacrifices. The result was a powerful conviction on the part of many Shakers that their way of life was the path to salvation. When asked why he was so cheerful, an aged Brother replied in 1851, "Why, I can't help it, for I love the way of God & keep my union to my Elders, & the Elders keep their union to the Ministry, & the Ministry are joined to Heaven; & how can I help being happy?"

The stone wall bordering the field south of the Meetinghouse at Canterbury, New Hampshire, was built in 1793 of large blocks of granite hauled into place, probably by teams of oxen. Some of the rocks are more than a yard across. The face of the wall is remarkably flat—an accomplishment indeed, considering the size of the stones. The stone wall is like an emblem of the community itself—the fitting together of different parts to make a whole more valuable than the sum of the individual parts. In the background is the Meetinghouse, built in 1792 as a joint effort by members of the newly established Shaker community.

The Meetinghouse at New Lebanon, New York, was the largest and most impressive Shaker house of worship—and the mother church for the entire Shaker society. Here, up to 500 Believers and as many as 1,000 visitors gathered for public meetings on Sundays.

This Meetinghouse was built in 1824 to replace the original, much smaller meetinghouse, which served as the model for other Shaker meetinghouses in New York and New England. Inside, the first floor was a vast open span sixty-five by eighty feet in area, uninterrupted by pillars, which would have interfered with the Shakers' impressive worship dances. The upper floors in an ell to the rear served as the quarters for the New Lebanon Parent Ministry, the two Elders and two Eldresses who were revered as the highest authority in the Shaker world. The barrel roof was designed to make possible the open span of the first floor.

The attic of the New Lebanon Meetinghouse shows the remarkable framing that makes possible the absence of pillars in the single large room on the first floor. A boardwalk spans the length of the building between the arc of the roof and the gentler curve of the ceiling below. A custom-made curved ladder, used to work on roof repairs, remains in the attic.

While art for its own sake was not acceptable to the Shakers because of its "uselessness," Believers encouraged the making of maps of their own villages. Such views and plans were useful for community planning, and perhaps also served a spiritual purpose as records of these heavens on earth.

In July 1836, George Kendall drew and painted this *Plan of The First Family, Harvard*, in Massachusetts. It shows the main street through the village running parallel to a "water course." Among the Church Family buildings are the gambrel-roofed Meetinghouse, two large gambrel-roofed dwellings, a school, and assorted shops, stables, and barns. Of particular interest is the hip-roofed dwelling in the upper-left corner at the edge of the orchard. The "Square House," as it was known, had been the home of the fanatical New Light preacher Shadrack Ireland before Mother Ann's visit. When it became clear to his followers that Ireland's promise to rise from the dead three days following his demise was not going to be fulfilled, they disbanded in disillusionment. Mother Ann stayed in the Square House during her prolonged visits to Harvard between 1781 and 1783. It is one of the few buildings extant in the United States that Mother Ann is known to have occupied.

In 1783, Mother Ann preached in the town of Hancock in western Massachusetts. The converts she made formally gathered into a community in 1790 on the adjoining farms of the Tallcott, Williams, and Deming families. By 1840, the village had nearly 250 members in six communal Families.

This view of the Church Family from the south includes, left to right: the Garden Tool Shed (a small outbuilding later moved to this spot); the large red Laundry and Machine Shop (c. 1800); the Meetinghouse (1790); the Brick Dwelling (1830); the brick Poultry House (1878); the red Tan House (c. 1840), where leather was tanned; and the Round Stone Barn (1826), with the 1939 Dairy Ell.

STREET

WATER COURSE

PLAN

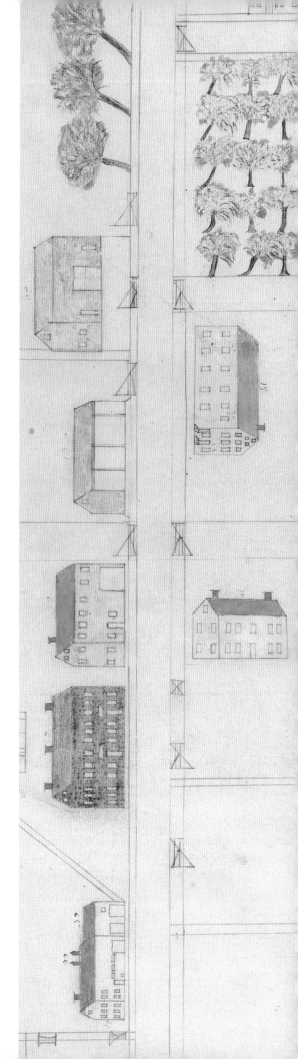

A plan of the Shaker village at Canterbury, New Hampshire, drawn in 1848 by twenty-four-year-old Henry Blinn (1824–1905), showed buildings, fields, orchards, and ponds in detail. This section of the large map, almost seven feet long, shows most of the Church Family buildings, which had been in existence for fifty-six years. Among the buildings represented are the dwelling for adults; a girls' house and a boys' house; a schoolhouse; a "sick house," or infirmary; an office for business transactions with the outside world; the gambrel-roofed Meetinghouse; the Ministry Shop; and a number of barns and workshops, including a spin shop, bake room, dairy, garden-seed room, doctor's shop, shoemaker's shop, joiner's shop, weaving room, distillery, herb-preparation shop, cider mill, printing shop, butcher room, blacksmith's shop, and tinker's shop.

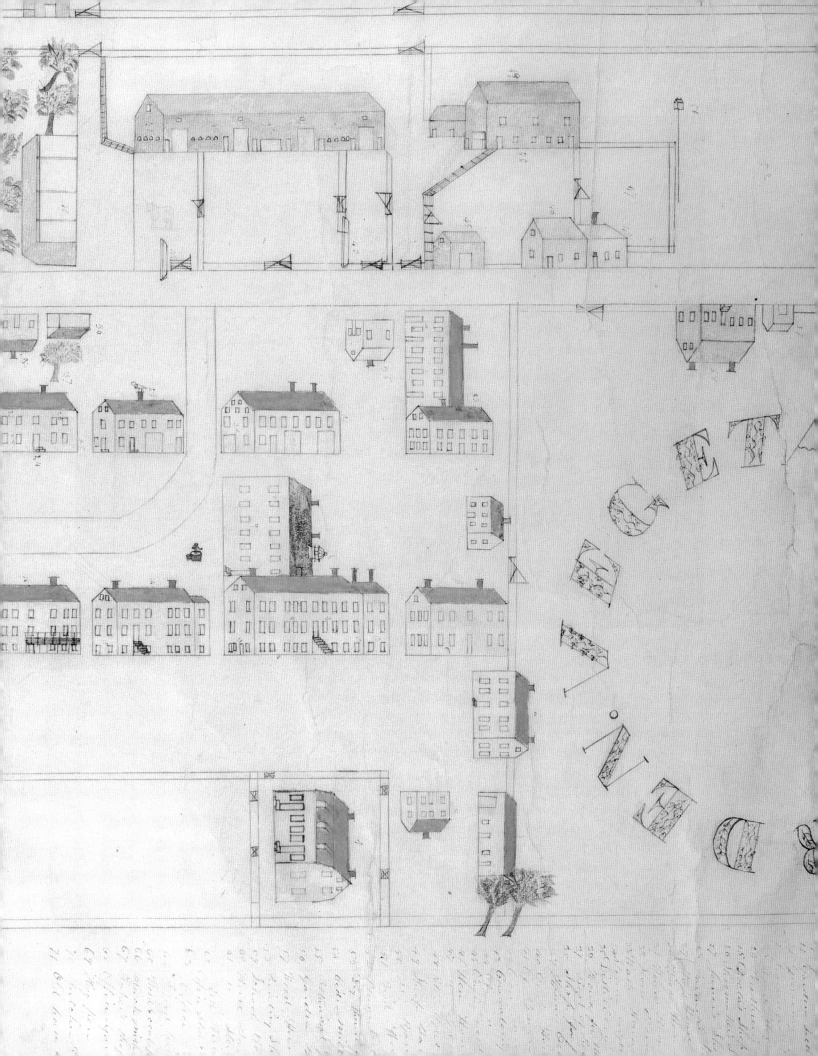

An easterly view between the Boys' Shop (1850) and Spin House
(1816) at Sabbathday Lake, Maine, highlights the extreme simplicity
of Shaker architecture. Although Shaker custom dictated that only
the Meetinghouse be painted white, Shakers in many communities
began to paint more of their buildings white in the late nineteenth
century, when they relaxed some of their strict rules.

Visitors found the Shakers' dwellings and work buildings unusually
large and hopelessly plain. Work buildings were customarily painted
red, tan, or yellow, with more costly white paint reserved for the
meetinghouse. Like Shaker architecture in general, this workshop at
New Lebanon, New York, is relentlessly unadorned—causing
Charles Dickens, a visitor to this community in 1842, to deride the
buildings as no more sightly than English factories or barns.

The handsome dwelling built for the Center Family at South Union, Kentucky, was started in 1822 and completed in 1833. In 1824, when the walls had been raised and the roof built, the date stone was set into place. The dwelling was the pride and joy of Elder Benjamin Seth Youngs (1774–1855), a versatile and able leader whose skills included clock making. The principal carpenter was Brother Robert Johns (1795–1863).

Although the dwelling was not designed with the customary double doors for Brethren and Sisters, it does have outside stairs that approach from different directions. The Brethren lived on the right side of the building, and the Sisters occupied the left. There are almost forty rooms on four floors. The ground floor or basement level has a kitchen, a dining room, a baking room, and six storerooms. On the first floor are ten "retiring rooms" and a large meeting room. The second floor also has ten "retiring rooms." On the top floor are several more "retiring rooms," a hallway referred to as the "Elders' Hall," and a very large attic.

In the mid-nineteenth century, Shaker societies began to build separate quarters for the two Elders and two Eldresses of the Ministry. Until that time, the Ministry had used the upper floors of the Meetinghouse. The new Ministry Shops, usually built next door to the Meetinghouse, were more spacious and more comfortable.

The Ministry Shop at Sabbathday Lake, Maine, was built in 1839 and enlarged in 1875. The Ministry Eldresses had their "retiring rooms" and workrooms on the second floor, and the Elders lived and worked on the first floor. Members of the Ministry, chosen for their ability and virtues, were among the most revered of the Shakers.

A detail of the back corner of the Herb House (1824) at Sabbathday
Lake, Maine, reveals a touch of economy. The building is faced
with clapboard on the front and both sides, all visible from the road,
but is faced on the back with plain shingles to save the cost of
clapboard and paint.

A corner of the Meetinghouse at Sabbathday Lake, Maine, shows
the characteristic angle of the gambrel roof and the dormer windows
that bring light into the upper floors, which were used as a
residence by the two Elders and two Eldresses who formed the
Maine Ministry.

The Center Family Dwelling at Pleasant Hill, Kentucky, remains one of the finest examples of Shaker domestic architecture. Like all Shaker buildings, it was based on American building traditions, which in turn came from English prototypes, and was then adapted to Shaker needs and made with precision and excellence.

The limestone dwelling was begun in 1824 and finished ten years later. Like most Shaker dwellings, it is divided into separate halves for Brethren and Sisters. Although the records are not clear, it is thought that the Brethren used the east side of the building and the Sisters, the west. Nearly a hundred members of the Center Family moved in when the building was completed.

There are more than forty rooms on a total of four stories. The basement level includes a kitchen, food-storage cellars, and a small dining room for the Ministry Elders and Eldresses. On the first floor is a communal dining room, one main kitchen and two baking rooms, a hall, six "retiring rooms," and two dressing rooms. On the second floor are six more "retiring rooms," two additional dressing rooms, a large meeting room, and four small rooms that constitute an infirmary. One of these is probably a physician's office, and the others are completely separate, possibly a measure taken to reduce the spread of any severely contagious diseases. The top floor includes two "retiring rooms," a skylit storage area with built-in drawers, and four smaller rooms for the storage of off-season clothing. At the very top, a curiously off-center cupola leads out onto a balustraded walkway on the roof, offering a handsome view of much of the village and the rolling bluegrass country.

A view from the steps of the Center Family Dwelling at Pleasant Hill, Kentucky, shows, from left to right, the Trustees' Office (1839), where visitors from the outside were welcomed and business was transacted; the Ministry's Workshop (1820), where the two Elders and two Eldresses in authority conducted their business; and the large white Meetinghouse (1820), where the Families gathered on Sundays for worship.

The Shakers at Sabbathday Lake, Maine, built this water tower in 1903 in the apple orchard high above the Church Family Dwelling. Water pumped up into it kept the community supplied. The availability of fresh water for drinking, washing, bathing, and water-powered equipment for large communal Shaker societies posed special problems that were met with ingenious solutions in different communities. In 1830, the Shakers at Hancock, Massachusetts, boasted running water on the first two floors of the Church Family's handsome new brick dwelling house. At New Lebanon, New York, the construction of a reservoir, an aqueduct, and other improvements occupied the Brethren throughout the nineteenth century. One Sister recorded their progress with tongue in cheek in 1895:

It seemed to uninstructed minds that Brethren must be playing
With instruments of various kinds, but lo! they were surveying.
Well then they figured, scored and planned on horseblock and on
      gate-post,
And always brought their board in hand when they to meals came,
      late most. . . .

They said with Grant, "We'll take this line," and not employ a
      plumber,
But we will lay the pipes ourselves if it should take all summer.
If man was made of dust, as said, we judged he must have floated,
But his descendants firmly tread when they with mud are coated.

62

The Church Family Dwelling at Hancock, Massachusetts, was built in 1830–1831 and housed nearly a hundred Believers when it was new. This vast building has forty-five rooms on six levels: a two-story attic; two floors of bedrooms, or "retiring rooms"; a main floor with public rooms, a Family meeting room, and a dining room; and a basement level with storage cellars and a large kitchen.

This view shows the east side, or Brethren's side. Visible on the left is the door into the small Ministry dining room, adjacent to the main dining room; the Brethren's main entrance is on the right.

Elder William Deming (1779–1849), the building's designer, described the new dwelling in 1832:

We commenced our building and in ten weeks from the placing of the first stone in the cellar the house was neatly laid up and the roof put on. . . . The work is all well done. There is none to excel it in this country. . . . We have found all the materials ourselves—such as sand, lime, stone & etc. with all the timber except the flooring. . . . Made all the windows, doors, cupboards and drawers, hung them and put on the trimmings. . . . With all this and a great deal more that we have done ourselves, the out expenses are about 8,000 dollars.

Added Elder William: "You will think our purse is pretty empty, which in truth is the case. But as we have given in obedience to our good Mother Ann's words—So we expect to receive. Her precious words were these, 'Your hands to work and your hearts to God and a blessing will attend you.' This we have found true."

The West Family Sisters' Shop, built in 1844, was one of the last major structures built at Pleasant Hill, Kentucky. Here, the West Family Sisters pursued their work, possibly making baskets, bonnets, or dresses. The building is noticeably old-fashioned for its time—its balanced façade carries on the Georgian tradition fashionable in the outside world decades earlier. However, the dormer and door are off-center, violating the otherwise strict symmetry, to fit form to function; the placement suits the interior halls.

Shaker communal life revolved around a strict schedule, with times for rising, dining, meeting, and working heralded by a bell. The system was much more practical than providing every member with a watch, or every workshop or "retiring room" with a clock. Tardy members who lingered in bed or on the way to a meal were called "old slugs":

A lazy fellow it implies,
Who in the morning hates to rise;
When all the rest are up at four,
He wants to sleep a little more.
When others into meeting swarm,
He keeps his nest so good and warm,
That sometimes when the Sisters come
To make the beds and sweep the room,
Who do they find wrap'd up so snug?
Ah! Who is it but Mr. Slug.

This bell, originally atop the dwelling house at the community in Alfred, Maine, was brought to Sabbathday Lake in 1967.

66

The second-floor hallway in the Church Family Dwelling at
Hancock, Massachusetts, separates the Brethren's bedrooms, or
"retiring rooms," on the left, from the Sisters', on the right. The bell
rope in the center brings to mind the imaginary but powerful line
that separated Shaker men and women. The Shakers were unusual
among celibate societies for housing men and women under one
roof—a situation that the Shakers attributed to the strength of their
vows. One Elder likened his sect to "monks and nuns, without the
bolts and bars."

The bell rope passes from the rooftop belfry down through six floors
to the basement kitchen, and can be rung from any floor—a
convenient step saver.

The dining room of the Church Family Dwelling at Hancock,
Massachusetts, features a pair of dumbwaiters, the design of Elder
William Deming (1779–1849), who was in charge of construction.
"The victuals is conveyed up [from the kitchen below] into the
dining room by means of two sliding cupboards," he explained,
pleased with the convenience of the arrangement. No doubt the
Sisters were pleased, too, at the saving of many steps at each meal.

The twin spiral staircases that rise through the Trustees' Office at Pleasant Hill, Kentucky, are representative of the simple splendors of Shaker architecture. The stairs soar through three stories and end in a skylit area. This building, begun in 1839 and finished in 1841, was an office where Shaker business leaders met with people from the outside world. Visitors could dine and lodge and transact sales, purchases, and other business.

Shaker dwellings usually provided a small separate dining room for the Ministry—the two Elders and two Eldresses in charge of two or three communities. Here, the Ministry's dining room adjoins the large dining room in the Church Family Dwelling at Hancock, Massachusetts. An outside door allowed the Ministry to enter and leave without passing through the dwelling's main hallway. Such measures were less privileges of leadership than a way of keeping the Ministry slightly removed from the communal Family so that it could be objective in counseling and disputes—in much the same way that officers in the armed forces remain separate from the rank and file.

The small trestle table, with its gracefully arching legs, was designed for this room. The Shakers favored trestle tables for dining because they gave the sitters more leg room. Believers did not make their own pottery, but bought dinnerware from the outside world, choosing plain, white undecorated china, such as this ironstone from England.

preceding overleaf:
Shaker dwellings had large meeting rooms where the communal
Family assembled for meetings on week nights or on Sundays when
bad weather made going to the community's central meetinghouse
impractical. Believers brought their chairs with them into the
spacious open room. This view shows one-half of the meeting room
in the Church Family Dwelling. When the dwelling was new, nearly
a hundred members gathered here. The room originally had two
interior wall panels that could be raised or lowered to divide the
room into two smaller rooms with a hall in between, providing
separate meeting areas for the Sisters and Brethren. The walls are
no longer extant, but the pulley system in the walls above remains
intact.

Shaker architecture in Kentucky is characterized by higher ceilings
and airier halls than cozier New York and New England Shaker
buildings. The high ceilings made sense in the warmer temperatures
of the South. The use of arches is also more typical of Shaker
buildings in Kentucky.

Here, a corner of the Center Family Dwelling at Pleasant Hill,
Kentucky, shows a closet with a transom window above to admit
light, and a Kentucky Shaker ladder-back chair, neatly hung upside
down on the pegboard to prevent dust from settling on the top of the
seat.

Visible at the end of the hall at the Center Family Dwelling at South Union, Kentucky, is the meeting room, with two wood stoves for use in winter. A particularly convenient feature of the banisters, perhaps inspired by a suggestion from the Sisters, is the raised base, which lifts the spindles above the floor to make it much easier to sweep or mop.

The dining room in the Church Family Dwelling at Hancock, Massachusetts, includes these characteristic conveniences—a built-in cupboard, probably for dining utensils, and a window in an interior wall to let natural daylight into the stairwell on the opposite side of the wall. The combination of wood and plain white plaster is also characteristic, as is the narrow strip of pegboard for hanging useful household items.

The stairwell, opposite, leads off the dining room to the basement kitchen. Two stovepipes join one of the main chimney flues.

According to Mother Ann's instruction, the Shakers used very simple place settings. "Never put on silver spoons, nor table cloths for me," she exhorted, "but let your tables be clean enough to eat from without cloths, and if you do not know what to do with them, give them to the poor." Believers used wooden or pewter dishes in their earliest years and later purchased plain white china, such as ironstone, from the outside world.

This view is of the small Ministry dining room in the basement of the Center Family Dwelling at Pleasant Hill, Kentucky; the main Family dining room is on the first floor. The Ministry customarily dined, lived, and worked apart from the communal Family in the interest of maintaining objectivity in guiding the community.

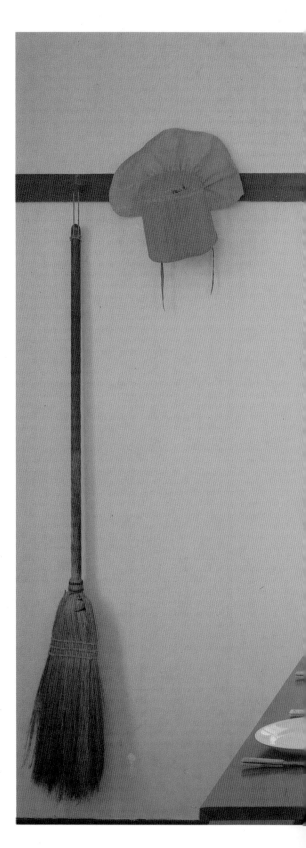

The two Elders and two Eldresses who composed the Ministry for a particular region devoted their lives to spiritual guidance and to overseeing the welfare of the communities in their care. They chose the Family Elders and Eldresses and generally saw to it that the communities ran smoothly and in harmony with the principles established by the Parent Ministry at New Lebanon, New York. Ministry members traveled frequently as part of their work, visiting New Lebanon and other societies as often as was practical.

A corner of the Shaker Office at the Fruitlands Museums suggests the Ministry's experience. The graceful trestle table, made at Harvard, Massachusetts, may have been a dining table for the Ministry there. Its relatively short length would comfortably accommodate four Believers; dining tables for the large communal Families were usually much longer. The wide pine top is made of two boards.

The remodeled Ministry Shop at Sabbathday Lake, Maine, featured several improvements in the new attic space provided when the original flat roof was changed to a pitched roof. This rack in a small closet was designed to accommodate off-season clothing. The ingenious V-shape allowed many garments to be stored in a relatively compact space.

The top two floors of the Church Family Dwelling at Hancock, Massachusetts, are attics, where the communal Family stored off-season clothing and bedding. This view shows the topmost floor and the stairwell down to the lower level. The Shakers liked to use skylights to bring natural daylight into their attics, in part to lessen the risk of fire from candles or lamps. In an adjoining room, a system of double skylights—one in the roof over one in the floor— lets daylight into the rooms of the level below. The simple elegance of the banisters and curved ceiling in a seldom-seen area of the building reveals the Shakers' attitude that perfection was important, even where it did not readily show.

In 1875, the Sabbathday Lake Shakers remodeled the original flat roof of the Ministry Shop, built in 1839, because it "leaked like a riddle" (or sieve) in the wet weather and hard winters of Maine. Elder Otis Sawyer reported that "the nuisance was taken off and a common double inclined roof put on, and finished off nicely which now affords for the Sisters much needed accommodation for storage." The two dozen large built-in drawers and cupboards above were used for general storage. The gray paint is original.

The attic of the Church Family Dwelling at Canterbury, New Hampshire, is one of the most impressive examples of the Shakers' preference for built-in storage. Called the "new attic" for 150 years since it was constructed in 1837 as an addition to the 1793 dwelling, the room has 2 under-eaves storage spaces, 6 closets, 14 cupboards, and 101 drawers, all beautifully made of clear pine and conveniently numbered. The attic was used primarily to store off-season clothing and bedding.

The storage area at the Church Family Dwelling in Enfield, New Hampshire, was equally impressive. That Dwelling, also built in 1837, featured 860 built-in drawers—about nine for each of the approximately ninety-five inhabitants.

This storage cabinet, with forty-eight drawers, was originally built into a workshop at Hancock, Massachusetts. Traces of original paper labels on the drawers indicate probable use as an herb-storage case, possibly in a pharmaceutical shop. The drawers graduate in height from top to bottom, a typical Shaker design feature that combines practicality with pleasing proportions—the larger drawers are at the bottom so that heavier contents are not precariously near the top. Although the case is as simple as possible, the play of drawer sizes and the punctuation of the darker drawer pulls make it attractive.

The Shakers were not the first Americans to build storage cupboards into their walls, but they did make extensive use of these conveniences in their dwellings and workshops. The built-in storage units in the Church Family Dwelling at Hancock, Massachusetts, are among the finest that survive. Elder William Deming (1779–1849), the building's chief architect, could not resist a little bragging about the workmanship:

Scarcely a knot can be seen in all the work, except for the floors and they are yellow pine and very good. There are 100 large doors including outside and closet doors; 245 Cupboard doors—369 drawers—These we placed in the corners of the rooms and by the sides of the chimneys. . . . And I think we may say it is finished from the top to the bottom, handsomely stained inside with a bright orange color.

The carpentry was shared by Brethren skilled at woodworking. Records and other evidence reveal that Brother Comstock Betts (1762–1845) made all the doors and that Assistant Elder Grove Wright (1789–1861) and Brother Thomas Damon (1819–1880) probably made the drawers. The drawers, with warm butternut fronts, are subtly graduated in height—with larger drawers at the bottom for heavier loads—the effect pleasing to the eye as well as practical. One advantage of built-in furniture was cleanliness—no dust could collect on top or underneath.

This Brethren's bedroom, or "retiring room," in the Church Family Dwelling at Hancock, Massachusetts, was nearly identical to nineteen other rooms that housed the communal Family. Believers shared their rooms dormitory-style, four or five to a room, and kept furnishings to a minimum for the sake of simplicity and order. Visible here are typical furnishings. At the far left, a built-in cupboard and case of drawers provided storage for clothing and other personal items. Other furniture includes a blanket chest with a drawer and a narrow bed for each occupant. The beds are on wheels to make them easier to move and to clean under. The cast-iron wood-burning stove, more efficient than a fireplace, was a typical feature of Shaker rooms. The long stovepipe helped to heat the room more uniformly.

Small, useful items, from left to right, include a string mop; a dustbox with a curved handle (a receptacle for swept dust); a round maple and pine spitbox, or spittoon, common in Shaker rooms before an early-nineteenth-century ban on tobacco; a small rectangular lap board, or lap desk, hung from a peg; a rectangular slab of soapstone under the stove, to heat the cold sheets on the bed; and a strip of blue rag carpet, easy to remove for cleaning. The cloth hanging on the pegs is based on a nineteenth-century print of a Shaker room showing fabric hanging on the wall—probably a form of insulation against drafts, as were tapestries in medieval castles. Other furnishings, not shown, would typically include a chair for each occupant, a washstand and looking-glass, and brooms and brushes for cleaning.

Education was an important part of life for children raised by the Shakers. By the early nineteenth century, Shaker villages had schoolhouses where young Brethren taught the boys in winter and young Sisters taught the girls in summer. Shaker schools were often considered among the best in their areas.

The Shakers at Canterbury, New Hampshire, were particularly progressive in teaching their young members. The first schoolhouse was built in 1823, then enlarged in 1863 with the addition of another story. To simplify the construction, the Brethren jacked up the original building and added the new story at ground level, saving the trouble of building a new roof. The Canterbury school remained in operation until 1934. In later years, local worldly children also received instruction in this well-regarded school.

The dining-room windows in the Church Family Dwelling at Hancock, Massachusetts, bring daylight into this spacious room from the east, south, and west. The Elder in charge of construction noted with pleasure that the building had 95 "24 lighted [paned] windows . . . in all 3,194 squares of glass including inside and out." The windows include a particularly ingenious feature: the sashes are held in place by a strip of wood on each side, fastened to the frame with three wooden thumbscrews on each strip. Loosening the screws allows the lower sash to slide up to any desired level, where it can be held in place simply by tightening the thumbscrews. The thumbscrews and strips could be removed altogether to bring in both upper and lower sashes for cleaning or repairing—a safety feature, especially in the high upper stories.

The Shakers commonly numbered rooms and storage areas for the sake of order; this wall of shelves in the Laundry at Canterbury, New Hampshire, is an example. Baskets of various shapes and sizes were used to carry linens and clothing to the Laundry for washing and ironing. Such baskets sometimes bore the initials of an individual member to help sort the clothes and household linens, which were also usually identified with initials.

preceding overleaf:

While the Shakers discouraged association between men and women on a one-to-one basis for the sake of celibacy, they realized that friendships between the Sisters and Brethren were natural and desirable. To this end, Father Joseph Meacham (1742–1796), a key Shaker leader after Mother Ann, instituted the "union meeting" in 1793. As described by a Brother in the 1850s, six to ten Sisters brought their chairs to a Brethren's room three nights a week to chat sociably. Propriety required a distance of several feet between the sexes. The meetings usually lasted an hour, with perhaps twenty minutes for singing, if desired. The participants were matched by the Elders and Eldresses, with rotations, so that no cliques could form or romances blossom. Reported one Sister in 1839:

Eliza and I have attended union meeting in all the rooms in the house once or more in a place. The brethren and sisters set about 6 feet apart and those that are rather hard of hearing appear as well contented as any one that can hear all that is said.

This room in the Church Family Dwelling at Hancock, Massachusetts, shows chairs lined up as if for union meeting. From a number of Shaker communities, they differ slightly in their details, but are remarkably alike. The wall clock, designed to hang from the pegboard, is one of six matching clocks made by Isaac N. Youngs (1793–1865) of New Lebanon, New York. Each of the clocks is dated 1840, although he did not finish this clock until seven years later. It was intended for a barn—a fact that gave Isaac pause for thought, raised as he had been on strict Shaker notions of simplicity. "It is rather a new idea to have clocks in barns, but they seem to be needful and admisable under suitable restraint," he finally concluded. Isaac signed his clocks modestly on the back of the face, unlike more worldly clockmakers.

Many examples of Shaker furniture point to shared use—sensible and desirable in a communal society. This double desk was made at New Lebanon, New York, in about 1840, probably for the use of Elders, Eldresses, or business leaders called Trustees. Small handwritten paper labels over the pigeonholes on the left specify *Letters*, *Quotations*, and *Religious Manuscripts*, among other designations. When closed, the desk presents a nearly flat front—the better to remain clean and dust-free. The pine desk retains its original light-orange stain.

Sister Aida Elam (1882–1962) of Canterbury, New Hampshire, shares wash day with a little girl, circa 1915. The Shakers took in and cared for thousands of children over the years, often developing very strong bonds of love. As the nineteenth century progressed, however, more and more children raised by the Shakers chose to live in the outside world when they came of age. With the passage of time and the establishment of orphanages and foster homes, there were more options for homeless children.

At Canterbury, New Hampshire, a group gathered for a photograph in the late 1880s. The young girls were not in Shaker dress. Elder Henry Blinn (1824–1905), a widely respected member of the community, sat on one of the large blocks of native granite that was used to terrace the lawn near the Dwelling. In the background on the left is the Ministry Shop (1848), where Elder Henry worked at various trades, including dentistry. On the right is the Meetinghouse (1792), by this time nearly a century old.

preceding overleaf:

In death as in life, the Shakers sought uniformity and simplicity. The earliest Shaker graveyards contained only plain wood or stone markers. Because of inconsistencies in appearance and cost, the community at New Lebanon, New York, decided in 1873 to authorize the replacement of old markers with cast-iron markers of a uniform shape and design. These were actually made for a few communities only, and the graveyard at Harvard, Massachusetts, is the only place where the markers remain *in situ*. Records show that 328 Believers were laid to rest here.

In keeping with the Shakers' preference for simplicity, their grave markers did not feature the tombs, urns, angels, death's heads, or vases of flowers popular in the outside world. The Believer's name, dates, and age at death were considered sufficient. Many Shakers lived long enough to occasion comment by outsiders. When questioned, the Shakers credited their longevity to their sensible living, their abstinence from alcohol and tobacco, and their celibacy.

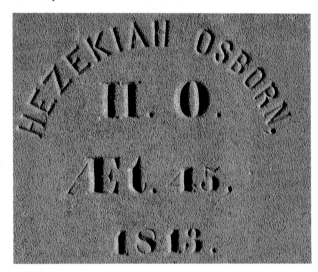

The early years in most Shaker communities were times of trial. Besides privation, the Shakers at Hancock, Massachusetts, suffered a severe loss in 1813, when many members died in a fever epidemic. Hezekiah Osborn, Jr. (1768–1813), who died at age 45, was himself a stonecutter. Later Believers added his name to the original stone, which was as simple as possible, bearing only his initials, age, and year of death. Later, the Hancock Shakers replaced the individual gravestones with a single large monument marked simply *Shakers*, to reduce graveyard maintenance and to symbolize their communal nature.

THE SHAKERS AT WORK

FROM THE BEGINNING, WORK WAS AN INTEGRAL part of Shaker life. Mother Ann Lee and her original English working-class followers did not have any source of income besides their own skills. As a young woman, Ann had worked in textile mills. Her brother William had apprenticed to their blacksmith father. Her follower James Whittaker was a weaver. After her arrival in America, Mother Ann repeatedly urged her listeners, "Put your hands to work, and your hearts to God, and a blessing will attend you."

The earliest Believers in the newly established communities brought with them a wide variety of skills and trades. Josiah Tallcott, Jr., of Hancock, Massachusetts, was a printer; Micajah Tucker at Canterbury, New Hampshire, was a woodworker and stonecutter; Thankful Goodrich at New Lebanon, New York, was a skilled seamstress. In time, the Shakers in various communities developed a remarkable number of occupations—tinsmithing, blacksmithing, spinning, weaving, dyeing, cooking, cabinetmaking, dairying, orchard work, beekeeping, masonry, carpentry, dentistry, medicine, teaching, basketmaking, butchering, gardening—producing much of what they needed as well as a wide range of high-quality manufactured goods for sale.

The Shaker label became synonymous with excellence. Humorist Artemus Ward poked fun at the Shaker way of life, but admired their applesauce nevertheless: "When a man buys a kag of apple sass of you he don't find a grate many shavins under a few layers of sass—a little game I'm sorry to say sum of my New Englan ancesters used to practiss." Even Charles Dickens, who disliked nearly everything about the Shakers, had to admit that their work was exceptional. "They are good farmers," he confessed, "and all their produce is eagerly purchased and highly esteemed. 'Shaker seeds,' 'Shaker herbs,' and 'Shaker distilled waters' are commonly announced for sale in the shops of towns and cities."

Because of their unusual way of life, which combined communalism

and celibacy, the Shakers had an approach to work that differed from their neighbors'. They had many more hands and were able to tackle more enterprises. Their farms eventually became much bigger than ordinary American farms; several thousand acres also provided each Shaker community with stone, timber, clay, and even iron ore in some communities. Most important, Shakers did not work competitively for private gain. Since all profits went to the group as a whole, workers did not receive individual financial reward for their particular endeavors. Their reward was of a different kind—the satisfaction of a job done well for its own sake. Despite the absence of the conventional monetary incentive, the Shakers were extraordinarily productive. Father Joseph Meacham summarized the Shaker philosophy of work and reward: "From each according to his ability, to each according to his need." Because money matters were handled by shrewd business heads in the Family's office, artisans were free to do their best without worrying about economic survival. In their unhurried but steady pursuit of excellence, Shakers followed the advice of Mother Ann, who had told Believers to work as if they had a thousand years to live, *and* as they would if they knew they were to die tomorrow.

With so many workers and so many jobs to be done, a system of organization was essential. Although considerations were sometimes made for an individual's special skills or preferences, the Shakers were expected to do what was needed for the good of the Family. Elders and Eldresses assigned permanent jobs and changes, while Deacons and Deaconesses were authorized to schedule temporary switches—during haying season, for example, a Brother who was principally a carpenter might be instructed to assist the farmers. Sometimes particular enterprises went along with positions of leadership. The Parent Ministry at New Lebanon, for instance, traditionally made baskets. With all the proper equipment, tools, supplies, and know-how already established in the Ministry's workshop, this practice made sense.

Although the Shakers valued virtuosity because they admired perfection, they also prized versatility. "If you improve in one talent," they said, "God will give you more." Most Believers were particularly skilled in one or two areas, but capable of fine work in as many as a dozen occupations. During the course of his life at New Lebanon, Giles Avery worked at building repair, masonry, plumbing, carpentry, plastering, teaching, cabinet work, wagon making, dipper making, orchard work, farming, and writing songs and journals; and he eventually became an Elder.

Sometimes assigned job changes were welcome—in 1852, Brother Henry DeWitt of New Lebanon rejoiced, "This morning I have heard the sound of liberty! Liberty from the bondage of old Boots and shoes; after having spent 26 years at the business." Isaac Youngs of the same community, who had loved fiddling with clocks since boyhood, worked as a tailor, as he was told, but when he was twenty-one, he finally got permission to work with an older clock maker, to his great satisfaction. Other changes were not so happy. In 1854, Anna Dodgson confided mournfully to her journal that her "long loved companion Maria" had been transferred out to take charge of the weaving department, ending ten years of happy work together. Some jobs were rotated on a regular basis; Sisters took four-week shifts in the kitchen, for instance, then moved on to other occupations.

The Shakers were far ahead of their contemporaries in believing that women and men were equal in ability and responsibility. Shaker Brethren and Sisters shared equally in leadership, an unusually progressive practice for the nineteenth century. When one visitor learned of the Shakers' acceptance of women as leaders, he was prompted to ask, "Suppose a woman wanted, in your Family, to be a blacksmith, would you consent?" The answer was an unhesitating no, because it would bring Sisters and Brethren into a relationship that the celibate Shakers did not think wise. Sisters and Brethren occupied separate workshops and were not allowed to enter each other's shops for longer than fifteen minutes without permission from the Elder or Eldress. Believers found that the traditional division of labor by gender was particularly suited to a celibate society. Sisters were in charge of the household, with tasks including cleaning, cooking, and textile work. Brethren were responsible for the farm and for the trades conventionally held by men. In times of need, Shaker men and women assisted each other with chores. One Brother wrote gratefully in 1837, "The Sisters have been so very generous as to turn out & top the beets," which were raised for cattle feed. "They are worthy many thanks." He had good reason to be thankful—they had finished 500 bushels.

Like other nineteenth-century Americans, Believers found that their work varied from season to season. Each month brought its particular tasks, and if the natural course of the farming year brought pressures—to get in all the hay before rain, or to harvest all the pumpkins before frost—it also brought a welcome variety.

In spring, Shaker Sisters occupied themselves with traditional spring cleaning, painting and staining interior woodwork, whitewashing the plaster walls, and clearing the dooryards of wood chips and other litter. In summer, the Sisters were busy with the vast kitchen gardens, picking and serving fresh greens and other fresh produce as they came into season. They also devoted their time to preserving stores for winter—making berry jams, pickling cucumbers, and drying beans and other vegetables and fruits. In fall, the principal tasks were harvesting apples and making cider, dried apples, and applesauce for winter use. Butchering took place in early winter, when freshly slaughtered beef and pork could be kept cool enough to retard spoiling, while the Sisters made salt and dried meat and stuffed sausages.

Textile work was also regulated by the seasons. The Brethren sheared sheep in late spring or early summer. The Sisters then processed the raw fleeces into fine homespun wool—washing, sorting, carding, spinning, and dyeing the wool as the year progressed. To make linen, flax plants were sown in spring and then pulled up by the roots in summer (to waste none of the valuable inner fiber). The plants were then rotted and pounded to free the fibers from the outer stem. The raw flax was then hatcheled, or combed, spun into fine linen thread, and bleached white for shirts, towels, and sheets. Short, leftover fiber, called "tow," was carded and spun into coarse brown tow cloth for work clothes and grain sacks.

In addition to their seasonal chores, Shaker Sisters were responsible for certain jobs all year long—including cleaning the dwelling daily, cooking and serving meals, washing dishes, and mending. Individual Sisters were also active in skilled professions, including teaching, weaving, nursing, and making goods ranging from pincushions and woolen cloaks to cheese and herbal medicines.

Brethren's work was similarly dictated by the seasons. In spring, Shaker men dressed the fields with manure, plowed, and sowed crops. Summer brought the long weeks of haying, and load after wagonload of freshly mown grass was drawn to the barns. In fall, Brethren joined Sisters to harvest apples and other crops. In winter, Brethren threshed the grain crops and cut, sawed, split, and stacked firewood. At New Lebanon, New York, 300 cords a year were required just to dry herbs for the community's pharmaceutical business.

Although nearly all Shaker Brethren had some farm work to do at some time in the year, many were also skilled in trades. Shaker "mechanics"—a traditional term for an artisan or a skilled handyman—built dwellings and workshops, made highways, laid stone walls, mended fences, dug drainage ditches, and produced useful iron, tin, and wooden items for home use or for sale. The mechanics often showed considerable ingenuity in making their work easier or more convenient, adapting worldly technology and frequently improving on it. "We have a right to improve the inventions of man," Father Joseph Meacham had said, "but not to vain glory, or anything superfluous." At least in one community, a certain distinction was made between the farmers and the mechanics. A young Brother at Enfield, New Hampshire, said that the word "farmers," in Shaker use, was "an appellation . . . as disreputable as 'rowdies' elsewhere." The farming Brethren, mostly young, vigorous outdoorsmen, had a great deal more freedom of movement and time because of the nature of their work, which required them to roam beyond the village and often to continue their work beyond normal working hours. (The young Brother added that the farmers cheekily referred to their stay-at-home indoor colleagues as "the Aristocracy.")

Today, much of the Shakers' work has vanished with their passing. The fields that the Brethren diligently plowed have grown back into woods, the fields marked only by stone walls that course incongruously through trees. The shirts and sheets that Sisters stitched have long since fallen to rags and disappeared. What does remain of Shaker work testifies to the makers' conviction that what they did really mattered. The humblest, most mundane objects—a coat hanger, a clothesbrush, a wheelbarrow—reveal a concern for excellence and grace. Many Shaker products are distinguished by a subtle beauty, derived from the simplest of elements: thoughtful proportions; graceful line; cheerful, bright color. Shaker barns, boxes, the lilting melody of the Shaker hymn "The Gift to Be Simple"—all reveal the gifts of the creators. Work and worship were not separated in the Shaker realm. As Eldress Bertha Lindsay of Canterbury, New Hampshire, says, "You don't have to get down on your knees to say a prayer. . . . If you're working, you can say a prayer."

This stone wagon mount was brought to the Fruitlands Museums from the South Family at Harvard, Massachusetts, early in the twentieth century. Stonecutters and stonemasons prepared foundations, steps, and fence posts in each of the Shaker communities. This graceful mount allowed Believers to enter or leave wagons or carriages in comfort and safety.

A stonecutter at Pleasant Hill, Kentucky, shapes a limestone dripstone, a fine reproduction of the Shaker original. The dripstones caught rain water from downspouts and carried it away from the foundation. It was typical of the Shakers to make such a mundane object so graceful.

Black converts were accepted as equals in Shaker communities. They were more numerous in Kentucky than in the North, but there were also some black Shakers in New York and New England, as well as a small Family of black Sisters in Philadelphia. While the Shakers did not fight in the Civil War because of their principles of pacifism, they did not support the institution of slavery. One Shaker Brother who had been born in Kentucky but raised at New Lebanon, New York, returned to his birthplace on a visit in 1852 and had "a pretty smart talk with a Kentucky slaveholder about the propriety or impropriety of holding slaves." Added the Brother, "He thought of course I was an eastern man, but I told him I was a Kentuckian by birth and yet could not approve of Slavery."

The Shakers in several communities made their own bricks. Here, the original mortar retains the lines scored by the bricklayer at Pleasant Hill, Kentucky. Although the Shakers built mostly with wood, they preferred stone or brick when they could afford it, to help prevent fires and to build for the ages.

right:

The restored Center Family Dwelling at Pleasant Hill, Kentucky, was made of native limestone, as was the original mortar. Modern masons duplicated the original bevel in the pointing between the stones—the outward angle sheds rain water and helps preserve the masonry.

This detail of a Shaker workbench shows what care the unknown maker put into a utilitarian piece of shop furniture. Shaker tools often reveal the same kind of care—testimony to the respect for honest work that Shaker workers felt. On this workbench, Shaker Brethren at New Lebanon, New York, are likely to have made all sorts of woodenware, from windows and doors to beds and chairs to boxes and pails.

The blue paint is unusual on furniture; it was usually saved for the interior trim of each community's meetinghouse. The workbench is made of mixed woods, including pine, maple, and oak or chestnut. The curved, unpainted shape is a sliding board jack, made of fruitwood. The bellying front is pleasing to the eye and also functional—it allows the jack to slide without hitting the drawer knobs. A vise on the left side of the bench, not visible in this view, holds one end of a board, and this jack holds the other end, which allows the worker to plane or otherwise work on the edge.

A cabinetmaker planes the edge of a board with the traditional tools and methods of Shaker craftsmen. "Put your hands to work and your hearts to God," Mother Ann Lee counseled her followers. Brethren who converted to the Shaker faith brought the skills they had learned in the world outside—carpentry, doctoring, tinsmithing, stonecutting, farming, printing, tailoring, and a host of other abilities. Younger boys raised in Shaker villages learned trades as apprentices to the older Brethren.

A cabinetmaker's shop with some early equipment is reminiscent of
Shaker woodworking shops at the turn of the twentieth century. This
shop, in a Shaker building at Canterbury, New Hampshire, is used
by a craftsman who makes fine reproduction Shaker furniture as
part of his work. Shaker furniture makers were typically versatile
workers who concentrated on cabinetmaking in the winter, when
farm work and woodcutting were minimal.

A splendid workbench testifies to the care that Shaker workers put into everything that they made, from tools and equipment to furniture to a meetinghouse. Several features distinguish this particular workbench, which is ninety-seven inches long at its oak top. It was designed and built for a left-handed woodworker—the bird's-eye-maple tail vise, ordinarily mounted on the right side, is on the left. The upper-right drawer has a pine lid and probably functioned as a handy writing or figuring surface—a stool pulled up alongside the drawer would make a good temporary "desk." An unusual and idiosyncratic construction feature in the drawers—sides that taper from thin at the top to thicker at the bottom (not visible in the photograph)—places this workbench among furniture known to have been made at Hancock, Massachusetts, or Enfield, Connecticut, in the mid-nineteenth century.

Shaker workshops were usually well supplied with the proper tools,
like this assortment of woodworking planes in a tool cabinet.
Believers were supposed to share equipment and supplies. "No one
should take tools, belonging in charge of others, without obtaining
liberty for the same, if the person can consistently be found who
takes charge of them," reminded the Millennial Laws of 1841.
"When anyone borrows a tool, it should be immediately returned,
without injury, if possible, and if injured, should be made known by
the borrower to the lender;—'The wicked borrow and never
return.'"

"Provide places for all your things, so that you may know where to
find them at any time, day or night," Mother Ann had counseled her
followers. Order was especially important in a communal Family,
since things were shared, not privately owned. This narrow wall
cupboard in the Brethren's Shop is pine, stained bright yellow in
part. It holds an assortment of awls for use in leatherworking and
shoemaking.

124

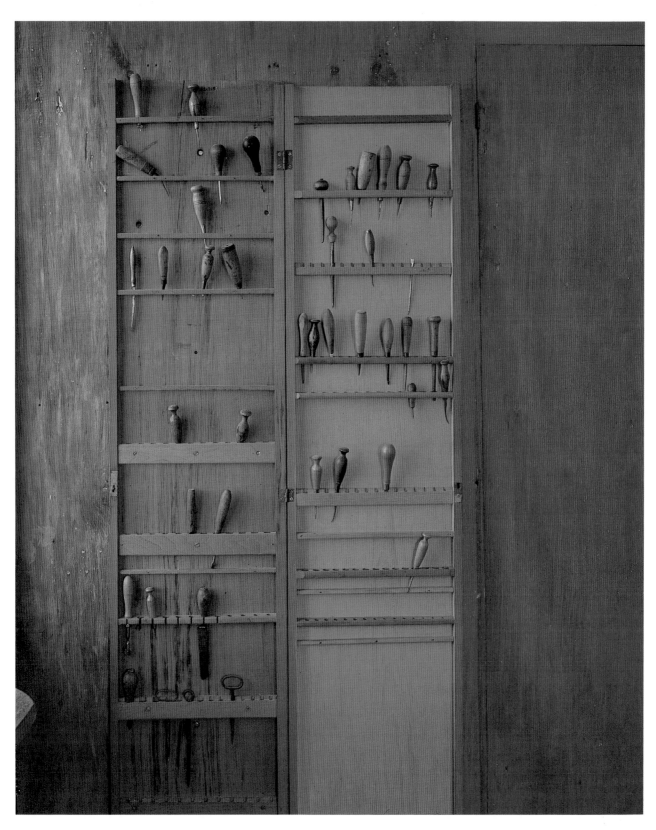

A basketmaker prepares splints of ash by shaving them to the
required thinness with a drawknife on a shaving bench—a
traditional technique. The Shakers of New Lebanon, New York, who
produced elegant baskets for their own use and for sale, developed
specialized machinery to speed the work without sacrificing quality.
In 1873, a Brother visiting from New Hampshire admired the
ingenuity of Elder Daniel Boler (1804–1892), who developed a
machine that planed the strips of wood. "Passing through a set of
rollers [they leave] the machine highly polished," he noted. "Most of
the basket wood is prepared in this shop—It forms quite a branch
of business for this family & several hands are engaged at it, most
of the year."

The basketmaker attaches a bail handle to a basket. This kind of
handle, and the single blue splint near the top of the basket, are the
adaptations of a modern craftsman to the traditional Shaker style.
Shaker baskets were pale, as is this one, when new; time has
mellowed them to a rich golden brown.

The Shakers used oak and ash splint, as well as willow, to make a wide range of baskets for home use and for sale. The basketmakers favored the use of practical features—such as the notched wooden handle here—while not necessarily innovating them. The notch grips the rim to prevent the handle from pulling away from the basket, even if it is filled with a heavy load.

This delicate basket, one of the finest examples of Shaker basketry, was designed with a lid that slides up and down the handle, but cannot be taken off—and hence mislaid. This kind of basket was often called a "feather basket" in the outside world, because the feathers or down of a plucked fowl were protected from blowing away. The body and the lid were woven over wooden molds to get their shapes. The design on the lid, called "twilling," required special skill.

The basket exemplifies the rule of thumb of Shaker design: don't make something if it's not useful; but if it is both necessary and useful, don't hesitate to make it beautiful, as long as the decorative elements are an inherent part of the design and don't interfere with function.

This practical, graceful oval wooden box is an emblem of Shaker work in general. The Shakers in several communities made boxes like this in a wide range of sizes for household and workshop use. These could hold anything except liquids. The distinctive finger-shaped joint on the side was not a Shaker innovation, but a tradition borrowed from the outside world and perfected. Cutting space between the fingers allowed the thin maple side to swell and shrink naturally with changes in temperature and humidity, with less risk of buckling than a straight seam. This box was probably the work of Elder Daniel Crosman (1810–1885), a master box maker at New Lebanon, New York.

"Trifles make perfection, but perfection is no trifle," said the
Shakers. The side of an oval box shows this attention to detail in the
curves of the fingers in the joint; in the careful alignment of the
small copper tacks (which will not rust and discolor the wood, as
iron would); and in the graceful shaping and pivot of the bail
handle.

A detail of the side of a finished oval box shows the graceful
repeating pattern of fingers, or "swallowtails," as they were called
by the Shakers, and the precise alignment of copper tacks.

134

Delmer Wilson (1873–1961) was the last Elder and oval-box maker at Sabbathday Lake, Maine. This versatile Shaker Brother worked variously as artist, photographer, orchardist, builder, barber, dentist, beekeeper, and woodworker. This photograph of Elder Delmer, standing next to a planer, was taken in his workshop in the Boys' House in 1915, when he was forty-two. He began making oval boxes in 1896 and continued well into the twentieth century, carrying on a tradition of more than a century in Shaker work.

Wooden dippers or measures were another useful Shaker product. They were used to measure dry substances, such as grain and flour, in quantities up to one quart. The dippers shown here remain in a wooden carrying device, ready for shipment and sale. Like the oval boxes, the dippers were formed of thin strips of maple that were soaked or steamed until flexible enough to be bent. The graceful handles were attached with rivets.

Examples of Shaker workmanship include a cupboard, oval boxes, and a pail. Shaker furnishings are characteristically free of ornament, but they are nevertheless appealing because of their shapes and colors. Believers liked bright, solid colors in their rooms, contrary to what outsiders have assumed. Products like these were made of local woods—pine for the cupboard and pail, maple and pine for the oval boxes. Shakers favored the use of plain wooden or white china drawer pulls, not the decorative brass hardware fancied by the outside world.

This Shaker shovel from New Lebanon, New York, carved from a single piece of walnut, was based on American traditions, but was noticeably finer and more elegantly proportioned than ordinary shovels. To prevent the danger of sparks from a metal tool, wooden shovels were customarily used in barns in which grain was stored. This shovel was repaired by the Shakers with a piece of tin when its bottom edge split.

An unusually large and handsome broom, probably made in a New York Shaker community, may have been designed for sweeping a wide hallway or a large meeting room.

The Round Stone Barn at Hancock, Massachusetts, is one of the spectacular examples of Shaker ingenuity and excellence. Although the Shakers did not originate the notion of a round barn, Elder Daniel Goodrich (1765–1835) adapted the idea in one of the biggest examples in America. The barn, 270 feet around, was built in 1826 to house more than 50 head of dairy cattle. Each of the barn's three floors is accessible from the ground by means of ramps. The top floor was for hay wagons, which drove in, circled as the loads were thrown into the center of the barn, and exited without having to back up or turn around. Up to ten wagons at a time could bring in hay.

The second floor was for the cattle, whose stalls ringed the barn's outer wall. A walkway between the cattle and the central haymow allowed Shaker Brethren to feed the herd with ease. (One visitor suggested that the Shaker cows' renowned productivity resulted from their clear view of all that tasty hay!) The ground level was the manure pit. Trap doors behind the stalls facilitated the removal of dung, which was brought out in spring to dress the fields.

The Hancock barn was the only Shaker barn that was round, but other, more conventionally shaped Shaker barns were equally impressive. The Shakers in Canterbury, New Hampshire, had a splendid barn 200 feet long, with polished chestnut beams. In New Lebanon, New York, a vast 5-story stone barn stretched 196 feet long by 50 feet wide.

The cow barn at Canterbury, New Hampshire, was one of the
highlights of the village. Built in 1858, the barn was 200 feet long
with 25-foot ramps at both ends, totaling 250 feet; it was probably
the largest barn in New Hampshire. The frame was made of
chestnut, and the barn was kept immaculately clean. Stalls on the
main floor, shown here, housed a large herd of fine cattle. The barn
was tragically destroyed by fire in 1973.

The interior of the Round Stone Barn at Hancock, Massachusetts,
shows the central haymow and the central shaft—a ventilating
device designed to bring fresh air into the hay to keep it dry and
reduce the risk of spontaneous combustion. In spite of great care,
the barn did catch fire and was rebuilt in 1864, thirty-eight years
after its construction. The Shakers decided to take advantage of the
misfortune by adding the clerestory with windows, which changed
the outline of the roof and allowed much more daylight into the barn.

At Canterbury, New Hampshire, a windrowing machine was
photographed raking hay near the Second Family Dwelling around
the turn of the century. Farming was the mainstay of the Shakers'
economy throughout their history. Shaker farms were admired as
models of good husbandry and productivity. Even critics of the
Shaker way of life praised the "sleek cattle upon their hills, their
excellent barns and outbuildings, their substantial walls and well-
cultivated gardens and fields."

Haying occupied Shaker Brethren for weeks during the summers. It was necessary to cut and bring in the hay in dry weather to prevent damp hay from igniting by spontaneous combustion. In August 1836, Giles Avery of New Lebanon, New York, recorded the completion of haying for the season with the last two oxen and two horse loads. The Sisters helped celebrate by bringing a treat of "some excellent drink sweetened with sugar & soured with lemon. . . . Also a large quantity of crackers cakes &c." Accordingly, the Brethren seated themselves "squaw fashion" around the goodies, although Giles noted that their appetites were somewhat reduced thanks to two similar visits by the Sisters earlier the same day. To prevent an attack of gout, the Brethren playfully decided to jump back and forth across the creek, and "went at it britches and boots."

These Canterbury girls busied themselves in a garden near the
Ministry Shop and Meetinghouse, circa 1915. In addition to
attending school and playing, Shaker children spent a considerable
amount of time doing chores. Eldress Bertha Lindsay, who still lives
at Canterbury, New Hampshire, was in charge of baking pies for the
communal Family of more than a hundred members when she was in
her teens, in the early twentieth century.

A worker leads a flock of sheep at Hancock Shaker Village in Massachusetts. Shakers here and in other communities raised thousands of sheep, including Merino sheep, which produce a superior fleece. The Shakers at Sabbathday Lake, Maine, still maintain a small flock and sell the wool.

overleaf:
The Shakers commonly used oxen for plowing and hauling. Oxen (neutered bulls) were stronger and calmer than horses. Most Shaker Brethren turned from various kinds of indoor work—furniture-making, coopering, and the like—to farm work in early spring as soon as the ground thawed, when the fields were dressed with manure.

Finished flat brooms from the broom shop at Pleasant Hill, Kentucky, are fine reproductions of the original Shaker product.

The familiar flat broom stands as an emblem of Shaker ingenuity and creativity. According to Shaker records, the first flattened brooms were produced by a Brother at Watervliet, New York, as an improvement over the traditional round bundles of broomcorn; the wider bottom edge swept more efficiently. Several Shaker communities went on to manufacture brooms and brushes in large numbers—an appropriate enterprise, given the Believers' devotion to cleanliness.

A well-made broom will stand on its own, before and after it has been stitched into the familiar flat shape. The bins behind hold broom handles. Turning these out in quantity kept Shaker Brethren busy at the lathe. Orren Haskins (1815–1892), a particularly gifted woodworker at New Lebanon, New York, went for the record in 1836. "[He] informs me that he has turned 1000 one day this week and I think now that all brags are beaten," wrote another Brother.

These fine reproductions of Shaker rocking chairs, made by the cabinetmaker at Hancock Shaker Village, Massachusetts, recall the way Shaker furniture makers frequently made things in multiples— several dozen ladder-back chairs for a new dwelling, for example, or a pair of washstands, or four small cases of drawers. Such production methods were not only efficient, but they helped to ensure uniformity—a quality the Shakers prized in their communal way of life, in which no person should have finer things than another.

At the same time, however, Shaker furniture makers did design individual pieces of furniture to suit a certain Believer's size; a rocking chair—like a suit of clothes—might resemble everyone else's, but it might well be extra large or small for a particular individual. Shaker Brethren usually made furniture in the winter months, when farm work was minimal. Most known furniture makers did a wide range of jobs during the course of the year. That their occasional products possess such grace testifies to their commitment to perfection in every kind of work.

These chairs rest on a Shaker workbench from New Lebanon, New York—one of the finest Shaker workbenches in existence. The top is made of three sections, using different woods for different areas. The first section is laminated maple or birch; the center, hard, durable oak or chestnut; and the third, a pine board, softer than the other hardwoods.

Shaker chairs were typically light but sturdy. This early example, probably made at New Lebanon, New York, in about 1820, is a streamlined version of an American rocker, with no carving or decorative painting to clutter its simplicity. The maker, however, was interested in making the chair look "right"—note the way the back slats increase in height as they go up. This subtle visual characteristic "balances" the chair in the eyes of the beholder and is typical of Shaker work—it goes beyond mere utility, but does not interfere with function. This unusually small chair was probably custom-made for a Shaker Sister. Some exceptionally conservative Shakers regarded rocking chairs as a needless luxury, but most enjoyed the soothing motion.

A detail of the rocking chair shows the woven tape seat, a close reproduction of original Shaker tape seats. Colorful, comfortable, durable, and easier to install than cane, rush, or splint, tape seats were used by the Shakers as early as the 1830s and seem to be a true Shaker innovation. Common seat patterns included plain checkerboards and a herringbone pattern, illustrated here.

A detail of the arm and front post of this rocking chair shows the type of construction typical of early-nineteenth-century Shaker chairs with arms. The entire front post was turned on a lathe from a single piece of wood—the broad "mushroom" at the top is not a separate, glued-on piece. This method made the front posts sturdy and unlikely to break or come apart.

157

158

A variety of colorful chair-seat tapes from Pleasant Hill, Kentucky, shows changes over time. The earliest tapes, on the left, were woven by hand by Shaker Sisters from home-dyed yarns; the earliest record of tape production dates from around 1820, when the Sisters were producing hundreds of yards a year. The tapes on the right date from the 1860s, when the Shakers found it more practical to buy twilled cotton tapes than to produce their own. "We used to have more looms than now," sadly reflected an Elder from New Lebanon, New York, in 1875, "but cloth is sold so cheaply that we gradually began to buy. It is a mistake; we buy more cheaply than we can make, but our home-made cloth is much better than that we can buy; and we have now to make three pairs of trousers, for instance, where before we made one. Thus our little looms would even now be more profitable—to say nothing of the independence we secure in working them."

The Shakers used colorful, comfortable woven tape seats in their
chairs as early as the 1820s. This is one kind of a simple tape loom,
used with an ordinary ladder-back chair to keep the warp threads
taut. The weft, or cross threads, will then be woven around the warp
to form a long tape. The Shakers also made small standing looms to
produce tape.

A Shaker ladder-back chair typifies the Shaker approach to life and possessions. Straightforward and unadorned, it nevertheless reveals features intended for comfort and convenience. The seat is made of woven cloth tape, more comfortable than splint or rush. The chair angles back at a slant to provide relaxed seating. The chair is light enough to be easily portable and to hang from the pegboard—a handy place to put the chair while sweeping. The chairs were commonly hung upside down, so dust would not discolor the top of the seats.

The back posts have a unique feature—wooden ball-and-socket "tilter" feet that keep the back legs flat on the floor when the sitter leans back. The tilters are held in place by narrow leather strips threaded through a hole in the foot and through a hole drilled in the leg a few inches above the foot. Such feet were becoming common on Shaker chairs by the 1830s. In spite of admonitions against leaning backward in chairs—"It is not right to lean our chairs back against the wall in our dwelling houses nor any decent buildings; nor against any beds or furnature," reminded the Millennial Laws of 1821—the habit persisted, and the practical Shakers adapted their chairs to suit. The main advantage was the protection of floorboards, most often made of soft pine, from the little dents that the hardwood legs of ordinary chairs would make.

Chairs similar to this were made by the thousands for the Believers in every community. These particular chairs were made at New Lebanon, New York, in about 1840.

Characteristic Shaker furnishings included built-in drawers and cupboards—these, in the Church Family Dwelling at Hancock, Massachusetts, are made of warm butternut and pine—and a cherry candlestand and maple rocking chair, both made at New Lebanon, New York, in about 1840. Based on styles popular in America around 1800, Shaker furniture was simple and refined, as well as light and easily portable—a plus for communal living, since all furnishings were owned by the entire society and liable to be moved around.

The finials, or pommels, atop the back posts of Shaker chairs were not merely pleasing to the eye, but also functioned as useful handles for lifting and moving the light, portable chairs. The finial shapes are often a clue to the origin of the chair, since the chair maker or group of chair makers in each village developed an idiosyncratic way of turning the finials on the lathe. This particular shape is typical of the work at New Lebanon, New York, in the mid-nineteenth century.

The thin lines circling the post are called "scribe" lines, and were marked to indicate where the slat should be inserted into a chiseled hole. Scribe lines are often found on the posts of Shaker chairs, although they were also used by chair makers everywhere.

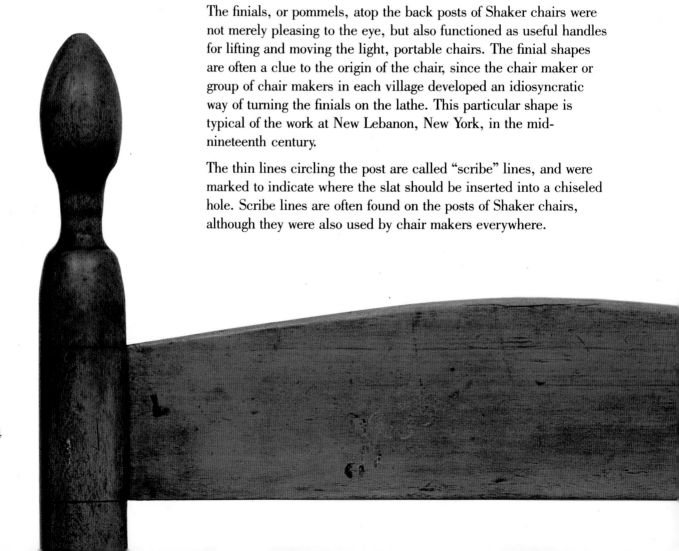

One characteristic of Shaker furniture is its delicacy. The legs of this drop-leaf table are very slender; the panels of the pine lap desk, or "writing box," are unusually thin; and the legs and spindles of the revolving chair are similarly free of excess weight. In spite of their delicacy, however, the pieces are surprisingly sturdy. Furthermore, they were treated with great care by Believers, who recognized in their possessions not private property to be abused, but communal property to be shared with future generations of Shaker converts.

All three pieces were made at New Lebanon, New York; the lap desk is stamped *1847*. Such desks were regarded as something of a luxury rather than a necessity by more conservative Shakers, for whom plain rectangles of pine sufficed as a writing surface. Chairs and stools with turning or revolving seats were made for the Shakers' use and for sale in the 1860s. One Brother visiting from Ohio admired the "new kind of chair, which turns on a screw pivot, every which way, different kinds and sizes."

A desk probably made by a Shaker Brother in Harvard, Massachusetts, is unusual for its visual "deception"—it looks like an ordinary case of drawers, but the front of the second drawer lowers to reveal a desk top. The construction is very impressive, with delicate dovetail joints in the drawers. Most Shaker furniture makers avoided anything that resembled deception, including veneer and grain painting (both of which made plain wood look finer and costlier). Perhaps it was furniture like this that prompted one very traditional Believer to complain on a visit to Harvard in 1850, "I think they have gathered into their habitations too much furniture which belongs to Babylon! Mother [Ann] used to say, 'You may give such things to the moles and the bats, that is the children of this world.'"

Examples of furniture attributed to the Shakers at Harvard, Massachusetts, include this cupboard and desk. The desk is a variation of the sewing desk, or "work stand." Of particular note is the way in which drawers are set into the bottom on the front and on the side. Such drawer placement is found on other Shaker sewing desks and furniture, a handy feature allowing the user to get things from the drawers without having to bend low under the work surface. What distinguishes this desk, however, is the addition of a writing desk on the front, apparently an alteration adapting the sewing desk for writing. Written journals were mandatory for certain Believers—including Elders and Eldresses, Deacons and Deaconesses, and Trustees—but ordinary members also kept diaries of their work and days, forming a rich record of everyday Shaker experience.

The sewing desk, or "work stand," was a popular item of furniture among Shaker Sisters in the years following the Civil War. The drawers provided convenient storage for small sewing implements, and the pull-out board handily enlarged the work surface without taking up extra space when the work was done. This exceptionally fine pair of sewing desks is unique because they were designed to fit together back to back.

The desks were made of birch, oak, and maple by Elder Henry Green (1844–1931) of Alfred, Maine, in about 1880. The design of these desks as a pair suggests the Shaker way of working—companionable, not lonely, with colleagues to share the work and talk.

Shaker Brethren often built sewing desks as special requests for individual Sisters. This desk was evidently made for Adeline Patterson (1884–1968), whose name was chalked on the underside of the pull-out work surface in front. This desk is identical to another desk in a private collection. Shaker furniture makers commonly made pieces in multiples of two or more.

An unusually tall stand made at South Union, Kentucky, was probably used as a lectern—an ink inscription on the underside of the top indicates that it was a "Meeting Room Stand." It is based on examples of Shaker stands made at New Lebanon, New York, and other eastern Shaker societies, but it is a little more exuberant in the curve of the legs and the swell of the post—evidence, perhaps, of the distance between the model community at New Lebanon and this community, more than 1,000 miles distant.

175

This cupboard and broom serve as emblems of the Shakers' insistence on order and cleanliness. The cupboard is attributed to the Shakers at Harvard, Massachusetts, and probably dates from the late eighteenth or very early nineteenth century. This kind of raised panel in the doors was typical of American woodwork at that time, and is found on early examples of Shaker work. Visitors from the outside world were frequently impressed with the remarkable cleanliness of Shaker villages. In 1851, Nathaniel Hawthorne found everything so neat at Hancock, Massachusetts, that he said it was "a pain and constraint to look at it."

Personal cleanliness was important to the Shakers. "It is contrary to order for any slovens or sluts to live in the Church, or even for brethren or sisters to wear ragged clothes about their work," reminded the Millennial Laws of 1821. There was probably a washstand in each dwelling "retiring room," or perhaps, in some cases, a communal washroom for each sex on each floor of the dwelling.

This washstand, made at Hancock, Massachusetts, of butternut, pine, and tiger maple, is almost identical to another washstand dated 1850. The subtle flare of the top and splashboard is typical of Shaker work—something done to please the eye, without adding ornament, requiring extra time and skill of the workman. Above the washstand is a looking-glass designed to hang from the pegboard. According to Shaker rules, looking-glasses were to be no larger than twelve by eighteen inches, to discourage vanity.

A corner in the Church Family Office at Harvard, Massachusetts, shows some of the finest Shaker interior woodwork in existence. The Office, built in the early 1840s, has about forty rooms and dozens of built-in drawers and cupboards made of pine. The building has been a private residence since the early twentieth century, when the community disbanded and sold its property.

The sturdily built work table, more than twelve feet long, is so delicately proportioned that it appears much lighter than it is. The wheels, like those on Shaker beds, made moving the table and sweeping the floor easier. Wheels or rollers were commonly used by Shakers on large, heavy pieces of furniture.

Both the table and the built-in storage drawers show how the Shakers designed their rooms to be easy to keep clean. "There is no dirt in heaven," Mother Ann had said.

This small table has a very unusual kind of foot. The arches facing each other at right angles to the wall are not out of the ordinary— similar feet are common on the trestle tables that Shakers favored for dining tables. It is the *third* "toe" on each side, pointing out, that is so odd. The construction, also, is as curious as a Chinese puzzle. To deepen the enigma, an old photograph shows the table with the toes pointing in. Clearly, at some time, the whole was taken apart and reassembled. This work might have been done by the Shakers or by a later owner. The small item on top to the left is a book press.

The Shakers produced their own boots and shoes—sturdy leather for outdoor wear and fine cloth slippers for Sunday worship services, when hundreds of dancing feet stepped lightly on the polished pine floor of the meetinghouse. The village shoemakers custom-made shoes for individuals, as this variety of wooden forms, or lasts, indicates. (One surviving last has a thick leather "bunion" tacked to the toe to accommodate one poor Believer's problem foot.)

The low workbench, made at New Lebanon, New York, in about 1840, has a comfortable padded leather seat. Upholstery of any kind was exceedingly rare in Shaker furniture, although a few workshop stools and chairs had durable leather seats like this.

Sewing implements on a desk from Harvard, Massachusetts, include a "tomato"-shaped pincushion, made of satin and stuffed with wool; fabric cases for knitting needles and threads; a wooden form to shape emery-filled "strawberries" for cleaning and sharpening needles; and some examples of plain homespun Shaker cloth. The Sisters in many communities made the manufacture of such "fancy goods" an increasingly important mainstay of their Family's economy in the late nineteenth and early twentieth centuries. The term "fancy" is slightly misleading, as it referred primarily to quality, not to decorativeness. The Shakers did not produce goods for sale that they considered unfit for use at home.

A Sister's sewing notions included such equipment as this fine hexagonal-weave basket, a miniature of a full-size cheese basket that was designed to be lined with cheesecloth so that the whey could drain from the curds. This miniature version (with a lid, unlike the large cheese baskets) was simply a small, nicely made basket for indoor use in a workshop. The larger basket with the delicately curved handles was also for light household use, possibly to hold a pincushion and small scissors or other useful items. The spool is typical of Shaker spools; with a narrow center, it holds considerably more thread than the modern commercial spools familiar today.

Shaker Sisters in several communities made warm woolen cloaks for their own use and also for sale in the late nineteenth and early twentieth centuries. Adapted from the cloaks commonly worn by American women in the eighteenth century, the Shaker cloaks enjoyed popularity among worldly women for wear to the opera. The brighter colors—including pink, red, purple, bright blue, and green—were intended for sale. The hoods and cloaks were often lined with satin.

A weaver works at an overshot coverlet on an original Shaker loom at Pleasant Hill, Kentucky. The term "overshot" refers to a traditional style of weaving—here, the red woolen threads "overshoot" the linen warp to form a reversible pattern. This technique may well have been too worldly for some Shakers, who were supposed to use plain blankets and "comfortables." Shaker Sisters in all communities were heavily involved with textiles, from preparing thread and cloth, to cutting and sewing clothing, to making household textiles, including coverlets, sheets, towels, tapes for tying, and carpets.

"Hands to work and hearts to God," said Mother Ann. The Shakers believed that work is a form of worship. Here, a textile worker demonstrates the traditional way of carding wool, or combing and straightening the fibers in preparation for spinning on a wheel. The fleece is combed and fluffed between two wooden paddles set with hundreds of wire teeth. The resulting rolls are then spun into thread or yarn on a large spinning wheel. The Shakers prepared their own cloth from home-raised sheep and flax (for linen) well into the nineteenth century, even when commercial cloth was readily available.

The device clamped to the bench is a table swift, which Shaker Sisters used for winding a skein of yarn into a ball. The swift was not a Shaker invention, but the Shakers at Hancock, Massachusetts, improved on it and manufactured them by the thousands. Thumbscrews fasten the swift to a table or other surface, and hold the collapsible arms out while the swift turns, releasing the yarn as it's wound into a ball. When the work was finished, the swift folded up neatly (like an umbrella) for storage. Swifts came in three sizes and sold for the considerable sum of fifty cents in the mid-nineteenth century.

Two yarn reels attributed to the Shakers at Harvard, Massachusetts, reflect the Shakers' interest in mechanization and technological progress—as long as it did the job as well as or better than the old-fashioned way. Such reels were based on traditions from the world outside. They were used to wind and measure yarn or thread into skeins. The "squirrel cage" type, on the right, may be a later model, but the principle is the same.

Shaker tools and equipment, no matter how mundane, were
characteristically made with as much care as if they were furniture
for the dwelling. A three-legged yarn reel, made by Shakers in
Alfred, Maine, was used to wind and measure yarn into skeins. The
double coat hanger was designed to hang two garments, perhaps a
Brother's coat and shirt or vest. Neither device was a Shaker
invention, but both are typically well made. They are shown against
the original deep-blue paint in an upper floor of the Meetinghouse at
Sabbathday Lake, Maine.

192

Shaker spinning wheels were characteristically free of unnecessary decorative turning on the legs and spindles. Large or "great" wheels, such as this one, were used to spin wool into yarn. Spinning occupied many Sisters for many years. After the sheep were sheared, the fleece was washed and prepared for spinning by carding into long soft rolls. The yarn was either dyed or used as it was.

194

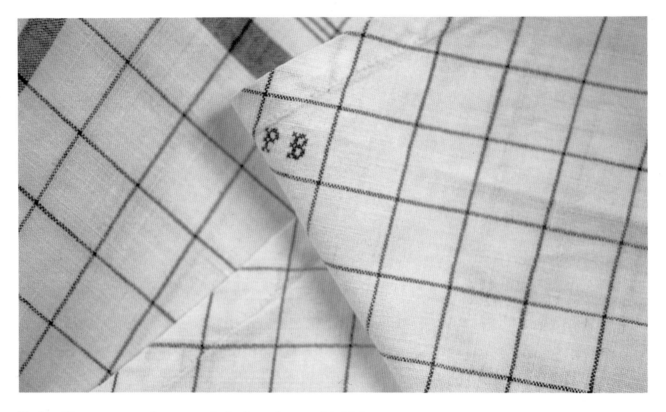

Shaker Sisters commonly cross-stitched numbers and initials on household textiles. While this was also common practice in the world outside, it made a great deal of sense as an aid in sorting laundry in the Shakers' large communal Families. Textiles, opposite, include an off-white woolen blanket, a white linen towel with an absorbent "diaper" weave, and a black-and-white checked kerchief. *No 1* may refer to a room number in a dwelling or to a number in a set of blankets; *67* probably refers to the date. The Millennial Laws of 1845 suggested, "It is considered unnecessary to put more than two figures for a date, on our clothes or tools, and it is strictly forbidden unnecessarily to embellish any mark." The initials *PB* stand for Peggie Bridges, a Sister at South Union, Kentucky, where these textiles were made.

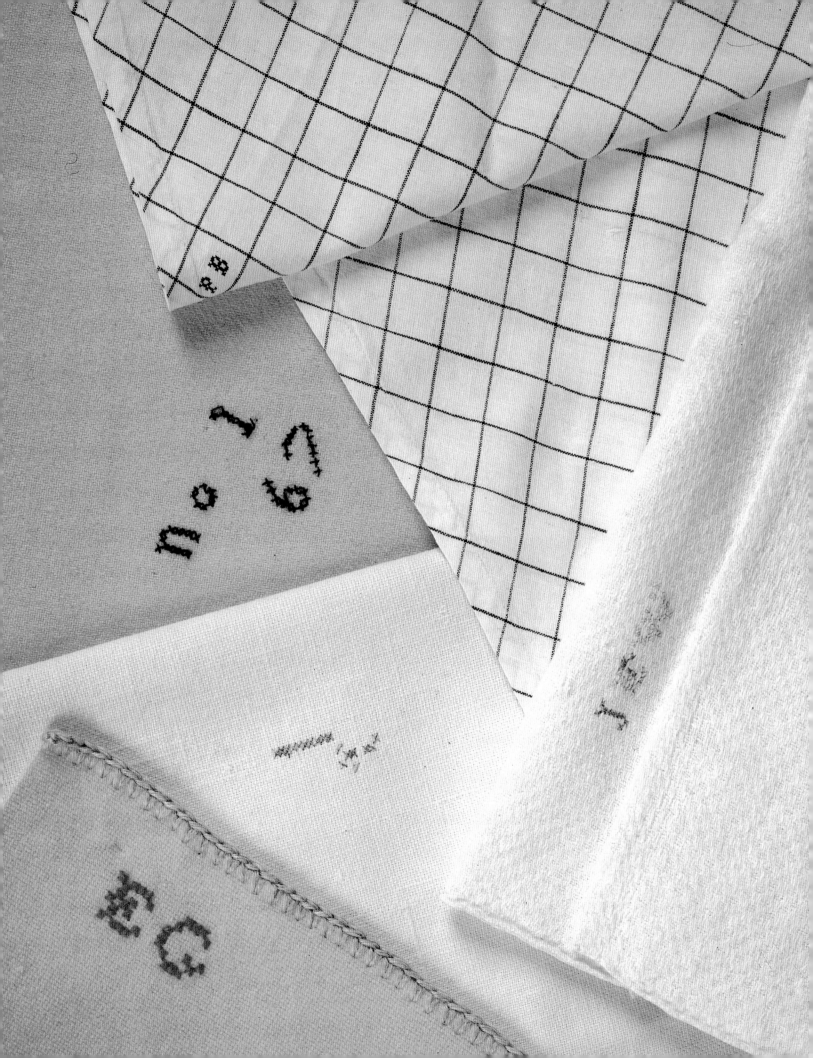

The Kentucky Shakers were among the early silk producers in the United States. By 1832, the Sisters at South Union, Kentucky, had produced enough silk to make themselves neck kerchiefs. These silk kerchiefs, made at South Union, show the bright colors that the Sisters favored. The iridescent appearance of the silk was created by using warp and weft threads of different colors—magenta and white to produce pink, for example. Weaving silk requires great patience because of the fineness of the threads.

Shaker Sisters dyed their homespun yarn and cloth in restrained but pleasing colors. The yarns here show the colors that result from traditional techniques of dyeing with plants and other natural materials. The Shakers were more likely to use dyes such as butternut, which yields a rich, dark brown, and indigo, a purchased dye that produces blue. Dyeing in a Shaker community was done on a large, almost industrial, scale and required considerable expertise. In 1849, some Sisters at New Lebanon, New York, ran into problems. Complained one:

O Sorrow & joy Betsy Crosman, Mary Ann Mantle, Amy Reed have finished coloring blue wool, they began the 12th had 105 lbs. & more than this had it all to wash over because Maria says we had such poor judgment & got the liquor too strong . . . & too hot I suppose. O Murder evry thing happens this awful year !!!!!!

The skeins of wool are, top row, left to right: a full skein (560 yards) of natural Leicester wool, and yarns dyed with osage orange and alum, tree lichen and alum, osage orange and copper sulphate, osage orange and cream of tartar; bottom row, left to right: hickory bark and copperas, cochineal, log wood and alum, madder root, and osage orange and copperas.

In 1879, the year after a new reservoir and aqueduct were built at Sabbathday Lake, Maine, the Shakers there installed a brand-new washing machine in the basement of the Sisters' Shop. Made of "polished stone"—probably soapstone—the washing machine weighed two and a half tons and required four horses to cart it from Durham, Maine, where it was made to order for the Shakers. An improved washing machine suitable for Shaker communal life and also for hotels and other institutions in the outside world was one of the few inventions patented by the Shaker society; it was designed and manufactured for sale at Canterbury, New Hampshire.

A hoist in the Laundry was an added convenience for the Shakers at
Canterbury, New Hampshire. On the hoist is a basket made at
Canterbury; the SXX mark on its side indicated that it was used in
the sweater trade. The Canterbury Shakers developed a good market
for their original "Shaker-knit" sweaters, mostly to New England
college boys, in the early twentieth century.

The Shakers at Canterbury, New Hampshire, installed a steam-drying room in their Laundry in 1854; until that time, all the clothes had been dried on lines. The room, with its sliding racks, was remodeled in 1862 and again in 1908, when a blower was put in the attic to force air up through the hanging laundry and out the ceiling through a pipe. Drying laundry inside, regardless of the weather, was practical for large communal Shaker Families, who could plan to do the washing on a predictable schedule.

Shaker Sisters were responsible for laundering the clothes and bedding for communal Families of up to a hundred members. It was not unusual for a Brother to assist with some of the heavy work. To speed up the job, the Shakers developed this stove, designed to heat dozens of flatirons at once. The stove was originally used in a laundry building at New Lebanon, New York. The Believers who used this convenience no doubt recalled that Mother Ann had supported herself during her first two years in the United States by taking in washing and ironing in New York City.

Wooden stocking forms were used to dry knitted hose to shape. The Shakers at Canterbury, New Hampshire, began to manufacture knitted stockings in the 1850s for sale to the outside world. These forms remain in place in the Laundry.

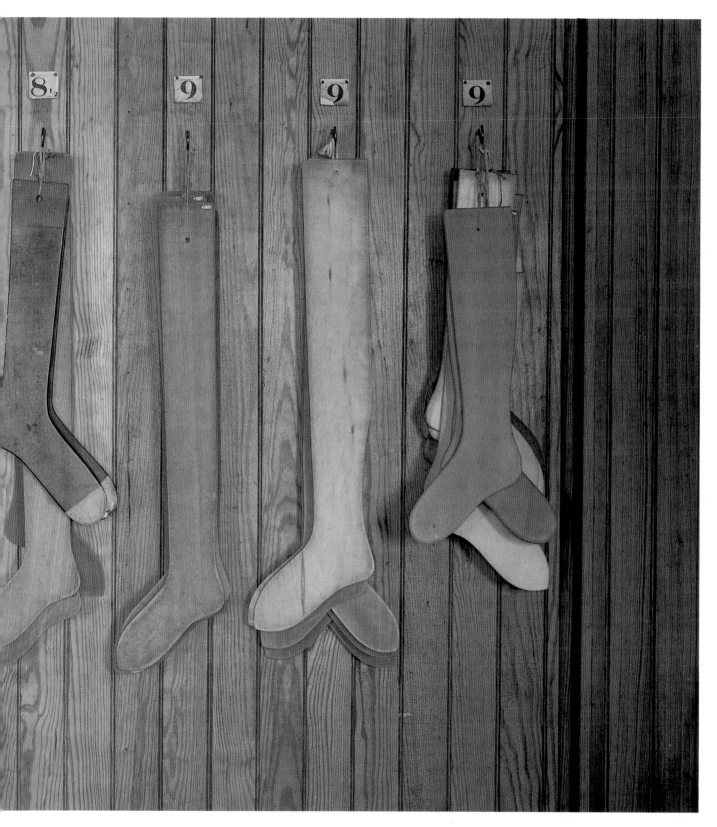

In 1849, Elder Hervey L. Eades (1807–1892) of Union Village, Ohio, and South Union, Kentucky, printed a large illustrated volume on Shaker clothing called *The Tailor's Division System.* It is believed that he sent a copy to each of the eighteen extant Shaker communities for the use of Shaker tailors everywhere. Today, the book is extremely rare. This plate showed tailors how to measure individual Brethren for "coats, vests, frocks, and trowsers."

Uniformity in all matters, including dress, was important to the Shakers. While there was some variety in Believers' work clothes during the week, depending on the kind of work they did, Sunday wear was uniform so that all members of each gender looked alike. Brethren's clothing was usually made by Brethren who were skilled tailors; mending was commonly done by the Sisters. The Millennial Laws of 1845 prudently cautioned Sisters not to mend or "set buttons on Brethren's clothes, while they have them on." Shaker tailoring systems were complex, derived from worldly systems and based on an individual's body measurements to ensure a precise, custom-made fit.

In 1924, Elder Delmer Wilson and the other Shakers at Sabbathday Lake, Maine, participated in the 150th anniversary of nearby New Gloucester with a flourish. According to his diary, the Shaker Family "fixed up banners at church and entered parade at old block House grounds. I got into big carriage wearing old Shaker coat, vest and broad brim hat. Were in parade two hours and no float drew more notice and applause than ours. Cameras were snapping in all directions." One such camera caught Elder Delmer in the traditional Shaker clothing of the century before. The plain coat, loose trousers, and broad-brimmed hat were based on styles popular in the outside world around 1800. By the mid-nineteenth century, such garb looked hopelessly outdated to worldly observers, but the Shakers thought it a waste of time to pursue endless changes of fashion. Although the Shakers have modified their clothing somewhat in the twentieth century, most of today's Shakers dress simply, in styles based on clothing worn by Believers in the last century.

212

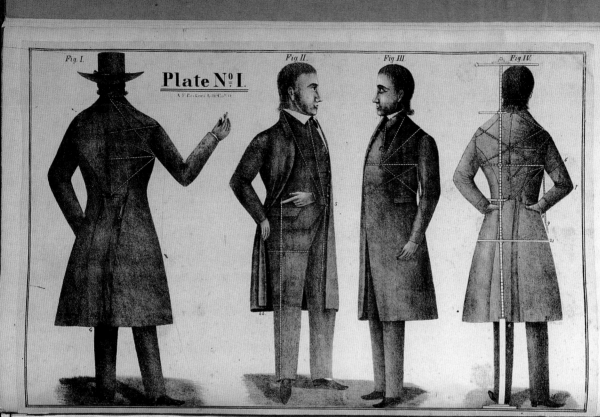

Plate N.º I.

Fig. I. Fig. II. Fig. III. Fig. IV.

MENSURATION.

DIRECTIONS FOR PLATE No. 1.

Rules of Measurement, for Coats, Vests, Frocks and Trowsers.

SURTOUT MEASURE, SEE FIG, 1,

Take your tape measure laid off in inches, ½ths & ¼ths.
1   Measure from 1 to 3 & 4 as length of coat.*
2   From 2 on back-seam, to the width of back, extend the measure to the elbow, and to the length of sleeve at hand; ☞ have the person to elevate his arm at right angles with the body, incline it a little forward and bend at elbow, sufficiently to determine the middle of elbow.
3   From 1 by front of scye on line A to 1.—This is called the Upper Shoulder Measure.
4   From 2 on back-seam over the shoulder, around by front of scye and back to 2.—This is called the Lower Shoulder Measure.
5   From 1 on line a a, round by front of scye, under the arm to back-seam.—This is called the Proof Measure.
6   From 1 on line a a, by front of scye, and down to waist at fig. 3.—This is called the Balance Measure.
7   Take lapelle measure from 1 over the shoulder or collar bone, extend it down to waist, hold it here with your right hand; with your left bring the upper end forward to collar point, as shown in fig. 2, for vest; then as low down as you wish your skirt to come.
8   Take the size around the breast and waist over the kind of garment, and set down your measure thus: with the name of the customer underneath:

16½, 38—19, 32—(26, 25½)—22, 24—22, 7½, 37—45, 34.
A. B.

* You will take all your measures over the kind of garment you are going to cut, except the frock, for which you measure over the vest; but in no case be governed by what the person has on, but be governed by your measure, which see to take correctly.

N.B. 1st. Select scales by the upper and lower shoulder measures, enclosed in parenthesis—always put the scale corresponding with the upper shoulder measure in the long arm of the Square, and that of the lower shoulder measure in the short arm. The scale of the upper shoulder measure, is to give the proportions up and down, or lengthwise of the garment; the other scale to give the proportions across the garment.

N.B. 2d. In order to find the right place for fig. 1, throw the tape across the person's neck, after turning up the collar—put your hands under his arms, taking hold of the ends of the tape, and draw it back and forth 2 or 3 inches—then dot with chalk under the edge of tape at fig. 1, for a starting point.

N.B. 3d. If the person's shoulders are not alike, or nearly so, you must measure both, and draft accordingly; and if you have difficulty in finding the centre of back at fig. 2, you will continue the measure round both shoulders, and set down half the measure, as shown on fig. 4; this is the surest plan to obtain the lower shoulder measure correctly, as it is sometimes difficult to find point 2.

JACKET, OR VEST MEASURE, SEE FIG. 2.

Let the person to be measured take off his coat—you then proceed to take the measure precisely as you do for coat, from 1 to 3 & 4 as length—you do not want sleeve measure.

Take the shoulder measures as for coat.
You take Lapelle Measure from 1 on line a, over the shoulder and down to fig. 5; hold the tape at fig. 5 with your right hand, and with your left carry the upper end forward to fig. 6, under the chin; then breast and waist measures, and set down your measure thus: with the name of the person measured underneath:

17, 24—(25, 24½)—21½, 24—22, 6½—36, 33.
A. B.

TROWSERS MEASURE, SEE FIG. 2.

Let the jacket be held back with the right hand, as the frock is; place the top of your measure, or fig. 1 of tape, on the top of hip bone, or as high as you wish the trowsers to extend. Let the person you are measuring, place the forefinger of his left hand on the top of the measure and hold it there, while you with the forefinger feel the crease of the muscle at the thigh bone joint, or "spring of seat;" note the distance as from 1 to 2, and the knee at 3, and bottom of ancle bone at 4. Now take the measure round the waist, hips, thigh, and knee; then set down the measure taken thus, with the person's name underneath:

11½, 24, 41½, (32, (37) 21) 14½.   A. B.

Now select scales by the waist and thigh measures, place the waist scale (32) in the long arm of the square, and the thigh scale (21) in the short arm, and you are ready for drafting.

FROCK MEASURE, SEE FIG. 2.

Let the person take off his frock or coat, but keep his vest on; you then commence at fig. 1, or socket bone of neck, and measure down to 44, as length; you then take the upper and lower shoulder measures and length of sleeve, and set down the measure thus:

40—(26½, 26½)—19, 33.   A. B.

You do not want proof, balance, breast, nor waist measures; proceed to draft as directed under Plate No. 10. You mark the right side of cloth on Frocks.

This fine linen shirt for a Shaker Brother was made at an unidentified eastern community in the mid-nineteenth century. The very long shirttail may have served as a kind of undergarment tucked inside the Brother's trousers, or this may have been a nightshirt. All the workmanship, from the homespun linen thread to the weaving and the stitching, is of the highest quality. The construction shows how straight coat hangers functioned well with traditional tailoring patterns. Note the cross-stitched initials and number near the bottom of the shirt.

The Shakers traditionally did not raise flowers for their beauty, but only for their use in medicines or for culinary purposes. Recalled Sister Marcia Bullard (1821–1899) of New Lebanon, New York:

The rose bushes were planted along the sides of the road which ran through our village and were greatly admired by the passersby, but it was strongly impressed upon us that a rose was useful, not ornamental. It was not intended to please us by its color or its odor, its mission was to be made into rose-water, and if we thought of it in any other way we were making an idol of it and thereby imperiling our souls.

Sister Marcia added that the roses were to be plucked with no stem at all, to avoid the temptation of fastening a fresh rose to a dress for adornment.

Rose petals were gathered and distilled into rose water, which was used medicinally and also as a flavoring in cooking, much as we use vanilla today. Rose water was a traditional ingredient in Shaker apple pies.

In the late nineteenth century and into the twentieth century, the Shakers relaxed their strict rules against ornamental gardens and cultivated beautiful flower beds.

The small but energetic Shaker Family at Sabbathday Lake, Maine, carries on several traditional enterprises, including the raising of sheep for wool and the raising and packaging of herbs and herbal teas. This herb garden abuts the Meetinghouse, visible in the background.

Equipment in the Farm Deacon's Shop at Pleasant Hill, Kentucky, recalls the Shakers' cultivation of medicinal herbs and plants. Typical equipment included scales, glass jars, and fine sieves, woven of silk, to process powdered ingredients. The long wooden box is cleverly designed with a curved bottom to rock like a cradle, sending seeds to one end and chaff to the other. The sieves and the box were made by the Shakers; the other equipment was purchased in the outside world.

Pharmaceutical equipment used by the Shakers includes a tin stencil for labeling containers of Shaker Hair Restorer—a product that promised to restore original hair color (like a popular modern formula), not to restore missing hair to a balding head! The Shakers, shrewd businesspeople, insisted on honesty in their advertising.

The Shakers in several communities were well known for their pharmaceutical industry. Believers raised dozens of varieties of medicinal plants in gardens of up to ten acres, and also gathered wild roots and barks from the surrounding woods and meadows. The plants were processed into extracts or were dried and pressed into small blocks that were wrapped in paper and sold. "They take great pains in drying and packing their medical herbs, and so highly are they valued that they have frequent orders for them from Europe to a very large amount," noted a visiting Yale professor in 1832. In addition, the Shakers also prepared medicines, including Tamar Laxative, a product of Sabbathday Lake, Maine, and Corbett's Syrup of Sarsaparilla, from Canterbury, New Hampshire.

One of twenty "retiring rooms," or dormitory-style bedrooms, in the Church Family Dwelling at Hancock, Massachusetts, shows typical features: wall pegboards, built-in cupboards and drawers, large windows, plain pine floors, and white plaster walls. The furnishings are similarly distinctive—unadorned, yet designed with care and sensitivity to line and form. The legs of the drop-leaf table splay slightly, as much for visual reasons as for the additional sturdiness; the legs of the candlestand flow in a graceful, streamlined echo of their worldly Chippendale roots; and the rocker's proportions are appealing. All the furniture was made at Hancock or nearby New Lebanon, New York, between about 1825 and 1850.

222

The Shakers prepared many of their own medicines from herbal ingredients for home use and for sale. Medicines came in liquid, powder, or pill form. This beautifully crafted device was used to make pills. By spreading a stiff medicinal paste on the grooved metal plate and sliding the crossbar forward and back, the worker sliced the paste into strips, which were then cut into individual pellets and dried. This exceptionally handsome pill maker was used at New Lebanon, New York, in the early nineteenth century. It may well have been bought from the outside world.

Each Shaker community had at least one infirmary, or Nurse Shop, where skilled Shaker physicians and nurses provided nearly all medical care. In times of emergency, the Shakers did not hesitate to call in a worldly doctor, but they were able to handle a wide range of services, from dentistry to appendectomies. When Shaker treatment did not relieve the complaints of aging Elder Grove Wright (1789–1861) of Hancock, Massachusetts, he let concerned Believers talk him into seeking relief at the "Water Cure establishment" at Saratoga Springs, New York, in 1860. "The first week appeared rather favorable for me, but after that, rather lost ground," reported Grove. "The Dr. thought, however, that if I would stay 6 or 8 weeks, he could cure me up." Added the Elder: "He probably thought I had money enough to last about that length of time."

In this room at Hancock, Massachusetts, specialized medical equipment includes, from left to right, a unique hospital bed, with cam arrangements to raise or lower the head or foot; a pair of crutches; and two adult-sized cradles for gently rocking weak or aged invalids. The movement was soothing, and it probably helped to prevent bedsores. Such cradles were not a Shaker innovation, but were adapted from worldly traditions.

Dairying was an important part of the Sisters' work in most Shaker communities. In a corner of the Sisters' Shop at Hancock, Massachusetts, tin milk pans and a large wooden butterworker occupy a corner of the Buttery. After letting cream rise to the top of the milk pans, the Sisters skimmed it off and churned it into butter. The grooved rolling pin in the butterworker pressed out any last traces of buttermilk to keep the butter from turning rancid. In 1863, one Hancock Sister noted the total amount of butter made in April, May, and June—875 pounds.

The Shakers made their own cheese. The addition of a piece of calf's stomach to heated milk produced curds and whey. Large, hexagonal open-weave baskets like these were lined with cheesecloth and filled with curds to let the whey drain off. At left, a cheese press—used to compress curds into round wheels of cheese, which were removed and stored for curing—stands on the floor.

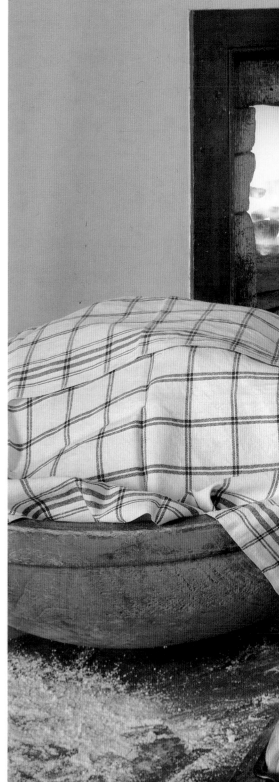

Shaker Sisters cooked in quantities that seem enormous compared with those of ordinary households. Dozens of loaves of bread were required weekly for communal Families of up to a hundred members. The size of the wooden bowl, here filled with rising bread dough, is typical. The flat wooden paddle on the wall is a peel, used to slide bread pans in and out of the deep brick oven.

Shaker women took turns in the kitchen, in shifts that averaged about four weeks. After their term, they went to other workshops to do other work. The large, cheerful kitchens must have been appealing to other Brethren and Sisters, because the Millennial Laws of 1821 offered these reminders:

All are forbidden to throng the kitchen or to go into it unnecessarily while the cooks are employed in it. Let no one attempt to instruct the cooks in their duty, nor undertake to represent the feelings of others, except those trustees whose business it is to direct them in their management of kitchen concerns.

A wooden firkin hanging in the Center Family Dwelling at Pleasant
Hill, Kentucky, reveals the maker's concern for utility and grace.
The container, designed to hang neatly from the pegboard, was used
in the Dairy for pouring milk. The edges are flared at the sides to
prevent spillage. The firkin was made by a cooper from wooden
staves like a pail or barrel, joined, and held in place with wooden
bands (the upper band was replaced long ago with a metal strip).

Preparing a chicken dinner for a communal Family of up to a hundred members required considerable advance time to kill, pluck, truss, and roast the bird. "We pick 35 chickens after breakfast," reported a Sister on kitchen duty in 1835, "& make some frost grape sauce." This chicken was roasted in a tin reflector oven, set before a hearth of glowing coals, and turned slowly with the handle connected to the spit. Near it are a tin colander and a stoneware preserving jar topped with a piece of tied cloth.

Shaker kitchen gardens—which might be as large as five acres—produced a wide variety of fresh vegetables for Shaker Families. The Shakers in several communities also developed considerable skill in preserving fruits and vegetables and making condiments, including applesauce, horseradish, and ketchup.

In 1843, the Shakers in New Lebanon, New York, printed *The Gardener's Manual* to share some of their know-how with the outside world, through "plain instructions for the selection, preparation, and management of a kitchen garden, with practical directions for the cultivation and management of some of the most useful culinary vegetables." The manual also served the purpose of advertising the New Lebanon Shakers' extensive and highly successful business of selling garden seeds; it included a list of seventy-four varieties, from "Asparagus, Giant" to "Turnip, Ruta Baga." The manual concluded with a few recipes for cooking and pickling garden produce. Perhaps its most valuable message was also its simplest: "The garden is said to be an index of the owner's mind." The neatness and fruitfulness of their gardens testified to the Believers' spiritual values.

Lemon pie—an extraordinarily rich concoction of sliced lemons and sugar in a crust—is a traditional Shaker recipe from Kentucky and Ohio. Shaker cooks prepared dozens of pies to serve to their large communal Families. In 1869, two Sisters at Watervliet, New York, recorded the results of their baking for a single month: "Made pies the first week 166, next 152, next 163, next 139, total 620." The two-pronged fork with the wooden handle is a pie lifter, for handling and moving hot pie plates.

OHIO LEMON PIE

Slice 2 lemons as thin as paper, rind and all. Place them in a yellow bowl and pour over them 2 cups sugar. Mix well and let stand for 2 hours or better. Then go about making your best pastry for 2 crusts. Line a pie tin with some. Beat 4 eggs together. [Alternate layers of lemon and sugar in an unbaked pie shell, then pour beaten eggs over all. Add top crust and cut small vents to let out steam.] Place in a hot oven [450° F.] for 15 minutes and then cut down heat [to 400° F.] and bake until tip of a silver knife inserted into custard comes out clean.

238

Angel food cakes were prepared in the kitchen of the Center Family Dwelling at Pleasant Hill, Kentucky, according to a traditional recipe. The first years in many Shaker communities were difficult, as large numbers of people struggled to produce enough to eat on what had been single-family farms. An aged Sister at Hancock, Massachusetts, later recalled the privation of her youth in the late eighteenth century:

Our food was very scanty, but what we had we ate with thankful hearts. For breakfast and supper, we lived mostly upon bean porridge and water porridge. Monday morning we had a little weak tea, and once a week a small piece of cheese. Wheat bread was very scarce; and when we had butter it was spread on our bread before we came to the table. Our bread was made chiefly of rye and Indian meal [cornmeal] mixed together. Our dinners were generally boiled. Once in a while we had a little milk, but this was a great rarity.

She concluded, "When I look back to those days, and then to the fullness with which we are blessed, it fills me with thankfulness."

The bounty of later nineteenth-century Shaker tables became well known to visitors and beggars. In 1886, a visitor to Hancock enjoyed a lunch of cold beef, white bread, brown bread, butter, boiled rice, baked beans, blackberry jam, blackberry pie, potato cake, apple pie, milk, pickles, cream cheese, cottage cheese, cake, and doughnuts—for a bill of 25 cents, cheap even at that time. He added that the cooking was "worthy of Delmonico's," a fashionable New York eatery.

240

The griddle and deep fryer in the Church Family Dwelling at
Hancock, Massachusetts, was a modern novelty when it was new.
With this equipment, the Sisters prepared pancakes, doughnuts,
fritters, and other treats. It was heated with wood fires in the
fireboxes behind the two small doors in the iron front.

The large brick oven in the Church Family Dwelling at Hancock, Massachusetts, accommodated dozens of loaves of bread or pies for a communal Family of nearly a hundred. In traditional fashion, the oven was readied for baking by building a fire inside. When the wood had burned to coals and the bricks were thoroughly heated, the ashes were scraped out, and the bread or pies were placed inside to bake. Since the heat could not be adjusted, cooks had to rely on experience to bake properly without burning or undercooking. A nineteenth-century Shaker recipe gives some idea of the quantities prepared:

SOFT GINGER BREAD

4 qts of Molasses, 2 [ditto] New Milk, 30 Eggs.
6 tablespoonfulls of ginger, 12 teaspoonfulls of pearlash, 10 cups of butter, [mix] about as thick as batter.

SPIRITUAL LIFE
AND WORSHIP

THE SHAKERS' RELIGION WAS NOT A ONCE-A-WEEK affair, but something to be put into practice in every part of their daily lives. As one Believer pointed out, "A man can show his religion as much in measuring onions as he can in singing glory hallelujah." Nevertheless, Sundays were special. This day was devoted to Family worship services and to private meditation. Mother Ann had insisted on setting aside mundane thoughts and tasks on the Sabbath, in order for Believers to fully reacquaint themselves with their higher purpose. In 1780, she told one prospective convert, "You must never cut your nails, nor scour your buckles, nor trim your beard, nor do any such thing on the Sabbath, unless in case of great necessity." By sundown on Saturday, all workshops were cleaned and put into order, all food was prepared for the simple Sunday meals, and all sins and troubles were confessed to the Elder or Eldress. Sunday was a day to refresh the spirit.

Of all that was remarkable about the Shakers in the eyes of the World, their method of worship distinguished them most. Instead of sitting quietly in church, listening to a minister preach, the Shakers all joined in dance, men on one side of the room, and women on the other, marching in unison to the sound of unaccompanied voices raised in song. While most visitors could understand the concepts of celibacy and communalism—after all, there *were* unmarried people in the outside world, and large nineteenth-century households and extended families experienced something akin to communalism—no one in the outside world got up in church and danced. It simply wasn't done. Outsiders were scandalized, amused, and usually critical. "Senseless jumping," declared Ralph Waldo Emerson, "this shaking of their hands, like the paws of dogs." James Fenimore Cooper sniffed, "It is scarcely possible to conceive anything more ludicrous, and yet more lamentable." An English lady described what she witnessed as a "swinging step somewhat between a walk and a dance," while the Shakers flapped their hands with "a penguin kind of motion."

246

To the Shakers, however, the unconventionality of their worship was its blessing. The dance gave them a vivid sense of "union," clearly visible in the uniform movements of hands and feet. Besides, the dance had its origins in the worship of Mother Ann and the early Believers, known in England as the "Shaking Quakers" because of the movements they made when under the influence of the Holy Spirit. In America, the first Believers experienced the same kind of manifestations. The first eyewitness description of Shaker worship, in 1780, reveals a powerful spiritual and physical energy:

> One will stand with his arms extended, acting over odd postures, which they call signs; another will be dancing, and some times hopping on one leg about the floor; another will fall to turning round, so swift, that if it be a woman, her clothes will be so filled with the wind, as though they were kept out by a hoop; another will be prostrate on the floor. . . . They have several such exercises in a day, especially on the Sabbath.

After the death of Mother Ann, Father Joseph Meacham had another inspiration. Instead of individual manifestations, he had a vision of a more orderly kind of worship. The "Hosts of Heaven" appeared to him, performing the simple, shuffling steps that the Shakers called "laboring." With this revelation, the true Shaker dance began. Later, Mother Lucy Wright encouraged Believers to speak out in meetings, sharing testimonies about their faith, and to sing lively hymns and anthems. Simple dance steps were added, including the "Square Order" and the "Sacred March."

By the early nineteenth century, the Shaker Sabbath had settled into a comfortable routine. Believers rose a little later than on weekdays and dressed themselves in their Sunday clothes. While work clothes varied with each Shaker's occupation, Sunday dress was strictly uniform, all Brethren attired exactly alike in striped trousers, white shirts, and blue vests; all Sisters, in white cotton gowns. In winter, Sisters wore dark gowns of "cotton-and-worsted," a blend of cotton and wool; Brethren similarly changed to their warmer winter dress of the same cloth. All Believers made the switch on the same day, to maintain uniformity.

Sunday breakfast was a simple meal, as were all meals on the Sabbath—perhaps baked beans or bread or other foods that could be prepared ahead of time. Worship meetings followed breakfast and noon dinner. The afternoon meeting was public, so visitors from the World could hear the message of Mother Ann firsthand. Depending on the weather and the season, each Family might stay at home to worship in its dwelling's meeting room, or it might join the other Families in the Meetinghouse. During cold or wet weather, Families usually stayed at home to worship by themselves. In the Meetinghouse, worldly spectators sometimes outnumbered the Shakers. When the new Meetinghouse at New Lebanon, New York, was dedicated in 1824, 500 Believers and 1,000 "World's people" filled the large hall. Even smaller communities attracted large crowds. In 1874, the Shakers at Sabbathday Lake, Maine, hosted more than 500 onlookers—so many that they did not all fit inside the room, and a "gaping crowd" surrounded the Meetinghouse to peer in through the windows.

The rest of the Sabbath was for private devotions. Believers did not go to their workshops or outdoors, but remained quietly in the dwelling, passing the day in companionship and rest.

Besides Sunday, other days of the year were regarded as holy. Thanksgiving was not originally a day of feasting among Believers, but a day for setting things right. On Thanksgiving Day, 1834, a New Lebanon Brother explained, "To day we keep according to the general custom of Believers, that is to clean up dirty places." Similarly, Christmas was a day for setting personal matters right, for "putting away hard feelings" in order to increase love and union in the community. Mother Ann's birthday—Leap Day by tradition, but celebrated on February 28 or March 1 as well—was like Christmas, a special day to recall the good example of the first Shakers.

By the 1830s, Shaker worship services had become a well-established American tradition. But in 1837, an event occurred that was to change Shaker life profoundly over the following two decades. At Watervliet, New York (Mother Ann's first Shaker home), two young Shaker girls began to receive communications from the spirit world. The phenomenon spread to other communities, as young people saw and spoke with angels and departed Believers, or received sacred songs in their dreams. It did not trouble the Ministry that the first evidence of "Mother Ann's work" appeared among the young. After all, Mother Ann had told her followers to be as simple and innocent as children. Soon, adults were also receiving messages, or "gifts," of song, new dance movements, and visions. Some Believers even received precious objects—balls of gold, shining lamps, gowns of silver cloth—no less "real" because they belonged to the spirit world and were visible only in the imagination.

Within a few years, the nature of Shaker worship and daily life had been transformed. As in the earliest years of Shaker life, individuals experienced widely varying "gifts." The Shakers were especially pleased when the mediums received messages from "primitive" spirits, who could thus be introduced to Mother Ann's message of salvation. In 1842, the Shakers at New Lebanon welcomed visits from "the Natives," or the spirits of an Indian chief and his tribe; the "Ice Landers"; the Arabs; and some Africans.

The Shakers in each community were instructed by divine revelation to establish outdoor "feast grounds," or holy places, to be marked with an engraved stone. Each Shaker village received a spiritual name—New Lebanon became "Holy Mount"; Hancock, Massachusetts, was known as the "City of Peace"; Sabbathday Lake, Maine, took the name "Chosen Land." By 1842, Shaker worship services had become so unpredictable that public services were suspended for three years, so that the Shakers could experience revelations without interruptions or distractions. (Charles Dickens, one of the first visitors to be denied entry, was keenly disappointed and was forced to base his derogatory remarks about Shaker worship on a popular print caricaturing the Shakers' dancing.)

The period of "Mother Ann's work" brought mixed blessings to the Shakers. Many sincerely inspired Believers contributed richly to a revival of the original Shaker values, especially simplicity, that were in danger of being forgotten as the Society grew increasingly prosperous. Talented Believers created a loving, beautiful legacy of songs and drawings. Older Believers in particular welcomed the revelations as a means of teaching the younger generation about the goodness of Mother Ann and the early Shakers. With the steady loss of "Mother Ann's first-born"—those who had known Mother Ann personally—the influence of Mother Ann, Father Joseph, Mother Lucy, and other bygone, beloved members was sorely needed.

But some individuals found an opportunity to turn circumstances to their own benefit by faking messages. Individuals who sought attention, who wanted power over their fellow members, or who were simply troublemakers could seriously disrupt Family harmony. One young Brother at Enfield, New Hampshire, pretending to be speaking in tongues, was found to be swearing in Latin. In 1850, Elder Freegift Wells confessed to questioning some revelations after a similarly bad experience. "I once swallowed down without doubting everything that came in the shape of a message from the heavens," he wrote. "But after a while I got confounded by receiving a message in the name of Mother Ann, which I knew was a positive lie! From that time I found it necessary to be more on my guard."

The revival faded in the 1850s, some twenty years after its beginning. Believers ceased marching to the feast grounds. The engraved stones were buried, and the sacred "gift drawings" were hidden away and eventually forgotten.

Shaker worship services underwent more change in the years after the Civil War. By the late nineteenth century, services consisted mostly of singing and speaking, and the dances were discontinued. Shakers in most communities began to gather in the Family meeting rooms in the dwellings instead of assembling in the Meetinghouse. As membership dwindled, and Families and then entire villages ceased to exist, the Shakers entered the twentieth century with quiet devotions. Although the public was still welcome to attend services, fewer and fewer visitors came.

Thomas Hammond, Jr. (1791–1880), was an especially gifted
member of the Shaker community at Harvard, Massachusetts. An
Elder of the Church Family, he also served as foreman of a chair-
making enterprise. He made, or was given, this clever five-pointed
ivory-handled pen to draw a musical staff with less effort.

Many Shakers composed sacred songs under what they believed was
divine inspiration. Such "gift songs" were created by the thousands.
The Shakers did not use musical instruments until late in the
nineteenth century, originally believing that the unaccompanied
human voice was properly simple and all that was necessary to
make music. From the mid-1830s through the 1880s, the Shakers
created a distinctive system of musical notation that did away with
the traditional staff altogether, using only letters of the alphabet and
other simple markings to designate timing.

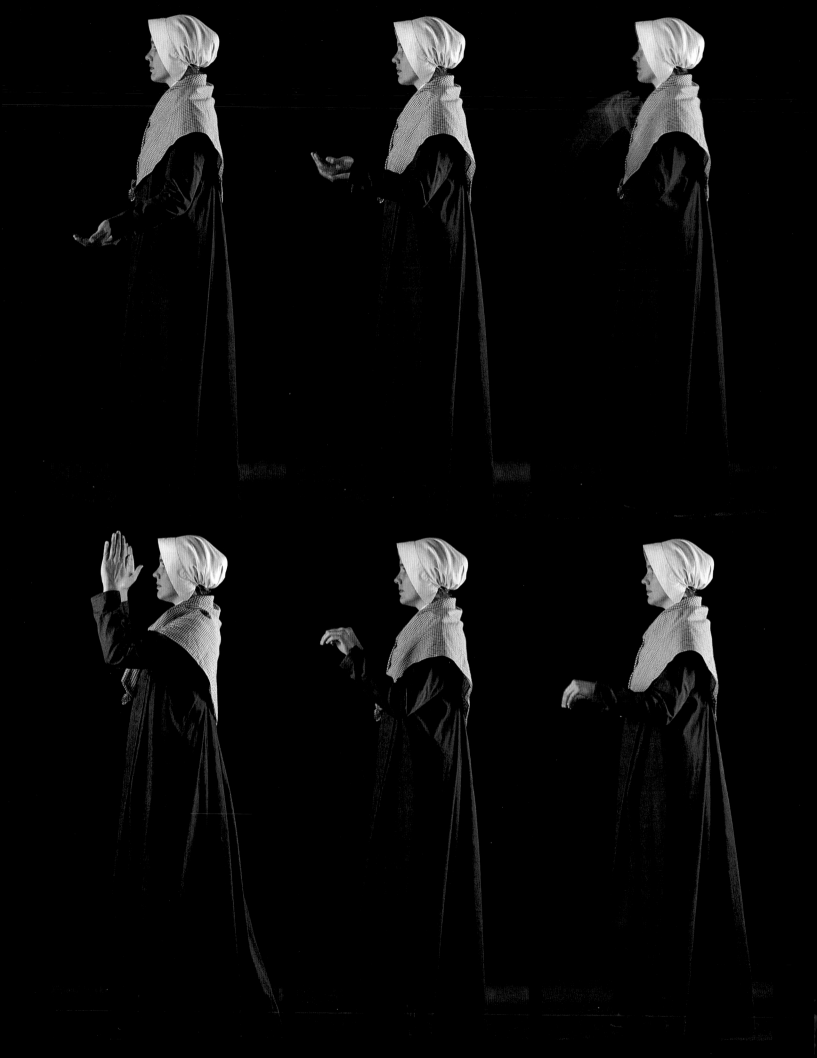

A museum interpreter in reproduction Shaker dress demonstrates the basic hand movements in the Shaker dance worship. With palms up and arms raising, she "gathers" blessings from her Brothers and Sisters. With palms down and arms lowering, she "dispenses" blessings. The most common Shaker dance was a very simple forward and backward stepping movement. Lines of Brothers and Sisters faced each other in the meetinghouse and moved in unison to the sound of singers' unaccompanied voices. The effect on visitors, who were welcome to attend worship for nearly all of Shaker history, was strong and varied. Some found the dances ludicrous; others admired the spirit of union that was so forcibly demonstrated as all Believers moved as one.

Shaker dancing began officially in the 1790s, when Father Joseph Meacham (1742–1796) instituted the dance as a more orderly alternative to the earlier Believers' manifestations of the Holy Spirit, including leaping, whirling, and shaking or trembling. Shaker tradition records that Joseph, although "entirely lacking in natural ability for the movements and exercises employed in worship," nevertheless devoted himself so earnestly to practicing—wearing the floorboards in his room smooth in the process—that eventually "he became endowed with such ability and grace that he seemed to exercise more like a spirit than a human being." No doubt his perseverance was inspirational to others.

The costume here, reproduced from mid-nineteenth-century originals, shows how completely the cap, neck kerchief, and straight gown conceal the figure—an intentional effect for the sake of modesty and celibacy. Fashionable visitors found both Brethren and Sisters hopelessly unstylish. Humorist Artemus Ward referred to one Sister as a "last year's bean-pole stuck into a long meal bag." In their turn, the Shakers ridiculed the fickle outside world, which seized on new fashions with every passing year.

overleaf:
The Center Family at Pleasant Hill, Kentucky, gathered on week nights to worship in the airy meeting room attached to the dwelling. The coved roof is unusual in Shaker architecture, although it may have been inspired by the curved roof of the 1824 meetinghouse at New Lebanon, New York. The arched transom window over the door is also unusual. The meeting room faces east and west, so it is filled with light all day long. When the Brethren and Sisters gathered to worship, they sat on portable benches or perhaps brought their ladder-back chairs from their "retiring rooms."

253

The Meetinghouse at Canterbury, New Hampshire, built in 1792, was the first building raised jointly by members of the newly established Shaker community. According to records, it was built in reverent silence, with no talking louder than a whisper.

In the background is the Church Family Dwelling, begun in 1793. Although it has been added to and improved many times in its nearly two centuries of existence, the basic original structure survives, making this the only Shaker Dwelling that includes portions of its original eighteenth-century structure. (More commonly, Shakers simply replaced their original dwellings with larger, more modern quarters in the nineteenth century.) As it exists now, the dwelling has about fifty rooms. The belfry, with a Paul Revere bell, was the subject of some consternation in 1837, when the visiting Ministry from New Lebanon, New York, found its appearance too worldly. To conform to acceptable Shaker standards, the Canterbury Brethren cut down the cupola by five feet and five inches to give it a more "modest" appearance. Today, the Dwelling is still used as a Shaker residence by Sister Ethel Hudson and her cats. The two other Shaker Sisters at Canterbury share another building.

The Meetinghouse fence at Sabbathday Lake, Maine, duplicates the prototype built at New Lebanon, New York, in 1841. An identical fence also remains in front of the Meetinghouse at Canterbury, New Hampshire. These fences illustrate the earnest desire of Shakers in all communities to follow the pattern of the society at New Lebanon, thought to be guided by divine inspiration.

Across the street in the background is the Church Family Dwelling, begun in 1883 and finished in 1884. The first meal served there was Thanksgiving dinner, 1884. The new dwelling replaced the original 1795 dwelling, which was moved from its original site with the help of more than thirteen yoke of oxen. The Church Family continued to live in its old home until the new structure was ready.

Beginning in 1837, the Shaker society experienced a wave of religious revivalism known as "Mother Ann's work." The purpose was to guide Shakers back to the example of Mother Ann and the earliest Believers to regain true simplicity and spirituality. During this period, Shakers received many "gifts" from the spirit world—messages and visions from angels, departed Shakers, and other revered figures, including even George Washington. Many messages came from the "Heavenly Father" and his female counterpart, "Holy Mother Wisdom," the Shakers' mother-father Godhead.

Several dozen "gift drawings" from the 1840s and 1850s reveal the inspiration of individual Believers. This drawing, featuring the "wings" of both heavenly Parents, is one of a series of nine similar drawings done in 1845 to 1847, possibly the work of Sister Sarah Bates (1792–1881) of New Lebanon, New York. According to the handwriting on the drawing, this represented "A Holy & Sacred Roll, sent from Holy & Eternal Wisdom brought by her message bearing dove to those who do, or may hereafter reside in the holy Sanctuary at Holy Mount." The vision was "given" in 1845 and "copied" in 1846. The detailed emblems and detailed inscriptions include a clock, trumpet, table, and lamp and five heavenly trees belonging to Mother Ann, her brother Father William, her faithful friend from England Father James, and her American followers Father Joseph and Mother Lucy—all figures of importance in the founding of Shakerism. Such drawings, haunting and mysterious today, are reminders of a time when the Shakers spoke with angels and saw Heaven in their dreams.

258

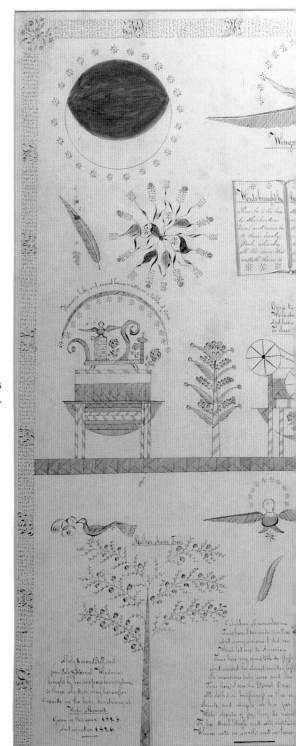

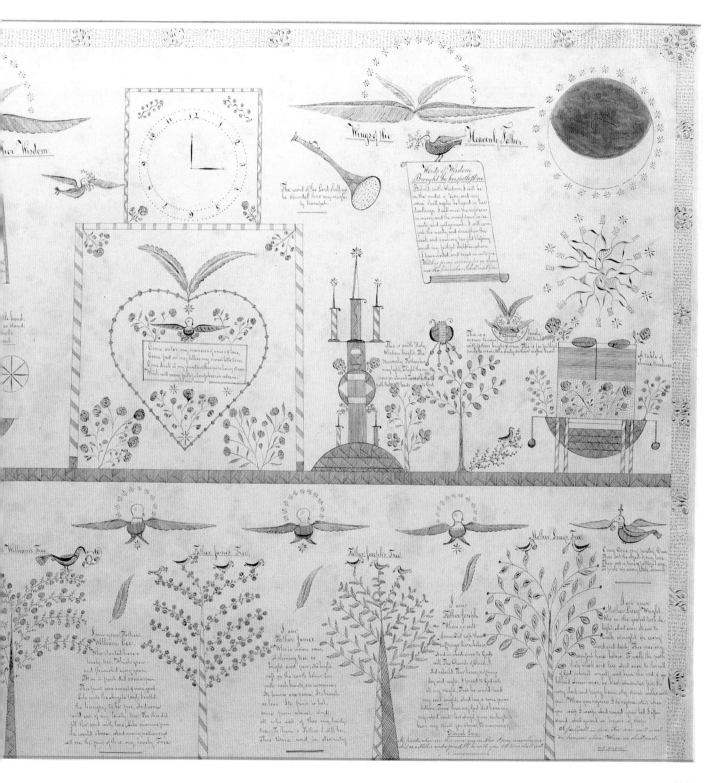

An Emblem of the Heavenly Sphere, attributed to Sister Polly Collins (1801–1884) of Hancock, Massachusetts, represented "A Present from Mother Ann," given in January 1854. The artist depicted her notion of Heaven, with forty-eight smiling saints and early Shaker leaders seated in neat ranks and all wearing traditional Shaker clothing. Mother Ann Lee, her brother William, and her faithful follower James Whittaker appear at the top with Christopher Columbus (whose role as discoverer of the New World, which became the chosen home of the Shakers, may have warranted his presence in such an honored position). Below Mother Ann, the Savior raises his hands in benediction.

The landscape of Heaven is lush with a wide variety of trees, from prosaic apple and peach to the more exotic "Celestial Cherry Tree" and "Tree of Order." Since Shaker villages were thought to be precise replicas of Heaven on earth, it's no surprise that Heaven, in turn, is furnished with simple Shaker furniture—two spindle-back benches, an arched-legged trestle dining table, and a writing desk and straight ladder-back chair.

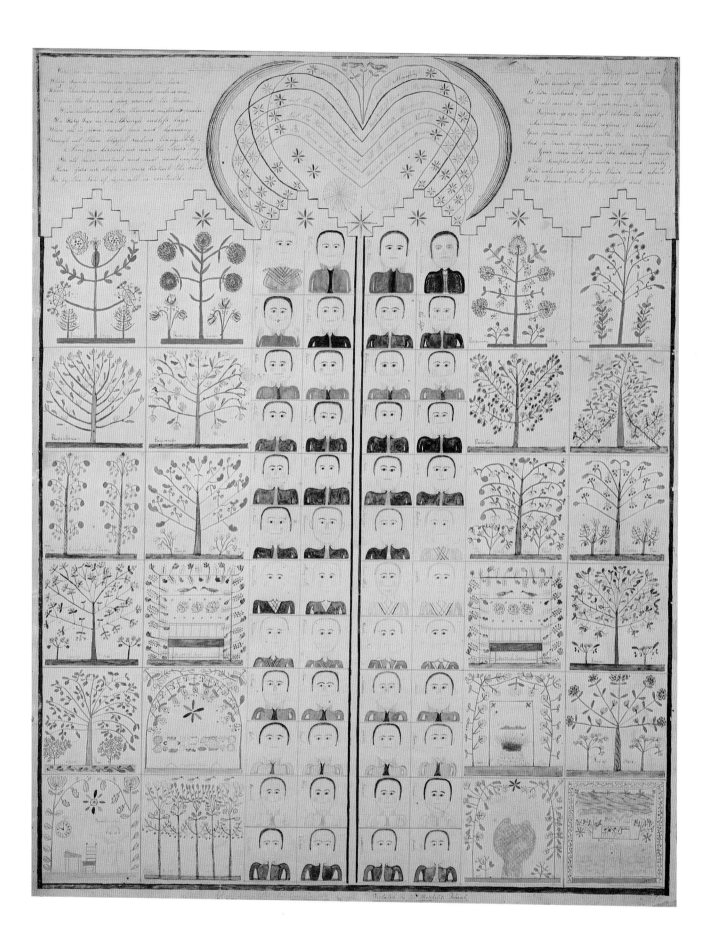

Another drawing attributed to Sister Polly Collins of Hancock, Massachusetts, is *The Gospel Union, Fruit Bearing Tree,* painted in 1855. According to the inscription, the artist's hand was moved when writing the text by the spirit of Elder Joseph Wicker, whose death three years earlier had left the community without one of the most active leaders of "Mother Ann's work" and its spirit manifestations. The tree, with its many varieties of fruit, was seen in the center of the meeting room in the Church Family Dwelling, sent as a gift from "holy Mother" via Elder Joseph's loving spirit.

262

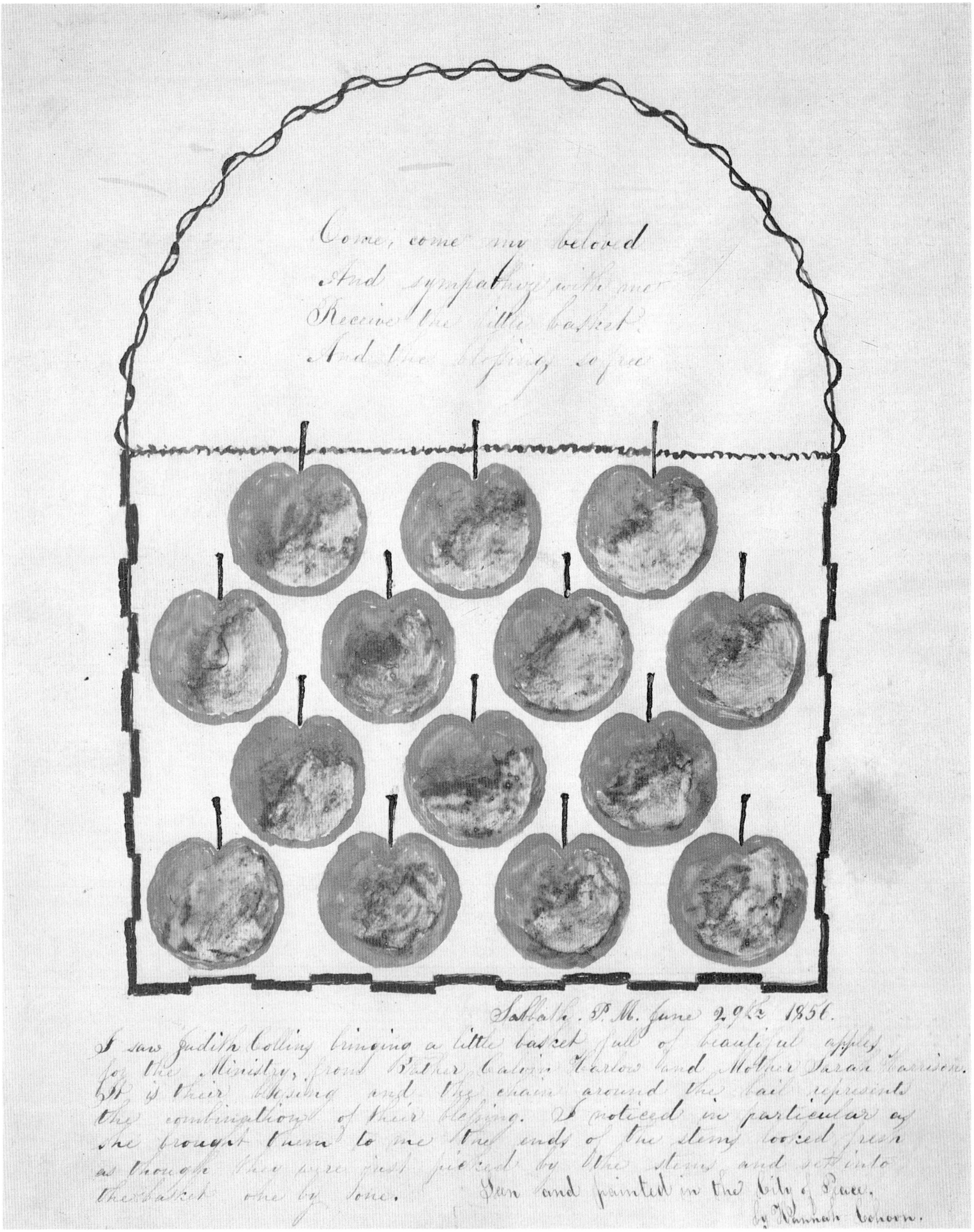

Come, come my beloved
And sympathize with me
Receive the little basket
And the blessing so free

Sabbath. P. M. June 29th 1856.

I saw Judith Collins bringing a little basket full of beautiful apples
for the Ministry, from Father Calvin Harlow and Mother Sarah Harrison.
It is their blessing and the chain around the bail represents
the combination of their blessing. I noticed in particular as
she brought them to me that ends of the stems looked fresh
as though they were just picked by the stems and set into
the basket one by one.   Pen and painted in the City of Peace,
by Hannah Cohoon.

264

Sister Hannah Cohoon (1788–1864) of Hancock, Massachusetts, best known for painting a striking *Tree of Life*, produced three other "gift drawings" that survive. Her last known drawing, *A Little Basket Full of Beautiful Apples*, is one of her most charming. Hannah was sixty-eight years old when she painted it in 1856. Intended as a gift for the Hancock Ministry, it was brought by the spirit of Sister Judith Collins from two of Hancock's most revered early leaders, Father Calvin Harlow (1754–1795) and Mother Sarah Harrison (1760–1796). "It is their blessing," adds Hannah's handwritten inscription, "and the chain around the bail [handle] represents the combination of their blessing."

overleaf:

The interior of the Meetinghouse at Sabbathday Lake, Maine, looks very much as it has for nearly two centuries. The beams retain their original handsome dark-blue paint. Blue paint, which was costlier and therefore more prized than shades like red or yellow, was so much a tradition in Shaker meetinghouses that the Millennial Laws of 1845 stated formally that meetinghouse interior trim should be painted "a blueish shade." To preserve the polished pine floorboards, Believers removed their ordinary shoes and put on cloth slippers for the dance worship. Portable benches, easy to move aside, and a floor uninterrupted by pillars provided a suitable place for the Shakers' impressive dances. Visitors from the outside world frequently commented on the extraordinary condition of the meetinghouse floors. One gentleman found the polished floors "elegant in spite of Shakerdom." An English lady declared one such floor "the best kept and most beautifully polished floor I have seen in this country," and added that spitting boxes for visitors' chewing tobacco were in every corner to prevent spots and stains.

The Sabbathday Lake Shakers still gather in the Meetinghouse to worship on Sundays. Although the Shakers have not included the traditional dance in their services for more than a century, visitors are still welcome to share in the speaking, praying, and singing.

Today, the Shakers in both remaining communities continue the traditions of the Believers who went before them. The Sisters at Canterbury, New Hampshire, observe the Sabbath privately. Primarily because of their age and health, they no longer deem it necessary to gather in the meeting room or Meetinghouse. The small Shaker Family at Sabbathday Lake, Maine, assembles in the Meetinghouse or meeting room. As always, visitors are welcome to share in the service.

As the Shakers stand now, poised on the threshold of their demise or their rebirth, they surely ponder their past as well as their future. Although numbers of people allowed the Shaker society to accomplish what it did, it is not ultimately *en masse* that Shakerism is experienced, but individually, in each Believer's spirit. When Mother Ann arrived in America, there were only nine Shakers. As the total number of Shakers in America comes full circle to fewer than a dozen, the strength of the society's existence is not diminished in its most real sense. As long as there is a single Believer, the Shakers believe that their way of life continues, agreeing with the Brother who wrote in 1837:

Those who're faithful just & true

Firmly speak it—I'll go thro'

And in answer not a few

Firmly say I'll go with you.

Tho' the number in the hive

Should be lessened down to five

I shall of this number be

Then we'll say so let it be.

SELECTED BIBLIOGRAPHY

ANDREWS, EDWARD DEMING. *The Community Industries of the Shakers*. Albany: The University of the State of New York, 1932.

————: *The People Called Shakers: A Search for the Perfect Society*. New York: Dover, 1953.

ANDREWS, EDWARD DEMING, and FAITH ANDREWS. *Religion in Wood: A Book of Shaker Furniture*. Bloomington: Indiana University Press, 1966.

————: *Shaker Furniture: The Craftsmanship of an American Communal Sect*. New York: Dover, 1950.

————: *Visions of the Heavenly Sphere: A Study in Shaker Religious Art*. Charlottesville: The University Press of Virginia, published for The Henry Francis du Pont Winterthur Museum, 1969.

BREWER, PRISCILLA J. *Shaker Communities, Shaker Lives*. Hanover, N.H.: University Press of New England, 1986.

CARR, SISTER FRANCES A. *Shaker Your Plate: Of Shaker Cooks and Cooking*. Sabbathday Lake, Maine: United Society of Shakers, 1985.

GORDON, BEVERLY. *Shaker Textile Arts*. Hanover, N.H.: University Press of New England with Merrimack Valley Textile Museum and Shaker Community, Inc., 1980.

HORGAN, EDWARD R. *The Shaker Holy Land: A Community Portrait*. Cambridge, Massachusetts: The Harvard Common Press, 1982.

KASSAY, JOHN. *The Book of Shaker Furniture*. Amherst: The University of Massachusetts Press, 1980.

LASSITER, WILLIAM LAWRENCE. *Shaker Architecture*. New York: Bonanza Books, 1966.

MEADER, ROBERT F. W. *Illustrated Guide to Shaker Furniture*. New York: Dover, 1972.

MELCHER, MARGUERITE FELLOWS. *The Shaker Adventure*. Cleveland: Press of Case Western Reserve University, 1968.

MILLER, AMY BESS, and PERSIS FULLER. *The Best of Shaker Cooking*. New York: Macmillan, 1970.

MORSE, FLO. *The Shakers and the World's People*. New York: Dodd, Mead, 1980.

MULLER, CHARLES R., and TIMOTHY D. RIEMAN. *The Shaker Chair*. Canal Winchester, Ohio: The Canal Press, 1984.

NEAL, JULIA. *The Kentucky Shakers*. Lexington, Kentucky: The University Press of Kentucky, 1982.

NORDHOFF, CHARLES. *The Communistic Societies of the United States*. New York: Dover, 1966.

PATTERSON, DANIEL W. *Gift Drawing and Gift Song*. Sabbathday Lake, Maine: The United Society of Shakers, 1983.

PEARSON, ELMER R., and JULIA NEAL. *The Shaker Image*. Boston: New York Graphic Society in collaboration with Shaker Community, Inc., 1974.

SPRIGG, JUNE. *By Shaker Hands*. New York: Knopf, 1975.

————: *Shaker Design*. New York: Whitney Museum of American Art in association with Norton, 1986.

SPRIGG, JUNE. PHOTOGRAPHS BY LINDA BUTLER: *Inner Light: The Shaker Legacy*. New York: Knopf, 1985.

WERTKIN, GERARD C. *The Four Seasons of Shaker Life*. New York: Simon & Schuster, 1986.

ACKNOWLEDGMENTS

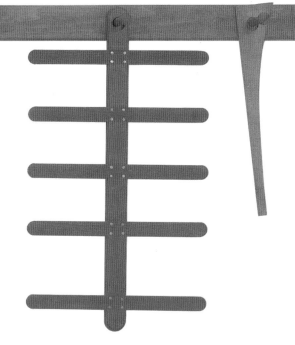

*We are grateful to these institutions
for their generous cooperation:*

Hancock Shaker Village, Pittsfield, Massachusetts

Shakertown at Pleasant Hill, Harrodsburg, Kentucky

Archives, Shaker Village, Inc., and the Canterbury Shakers,
Canterbury, New Hampshire

The Fruitlands Museums, Harvard, Massachusetts

The United Society of Shakers, Sabbathday Lake, Maine

Shakertown, South Union, Kentucky

The Shaker Museum, Old Chatham, New York

Old Sturbridge Village, Sturbridge, Massachusetts

Thanks also to those who posed for pictures:

Cheryl Anderson, dancer, Hancock Shaker Village, Massachusetts

David Lamb, cabinetmaker, Canterbury, New Hampshire

John McGuire, basketmaker, Hancock Shaker Village

Cliff Myers, boxmaker, Hancock Shaker Village

James Higgins and Jack Jenkins, stonecutters, Pleasant Hill, Kentucky

Martha Sue Mayes, cook, Pleasant Hill

Bianca Fiore, herbalist, Hancock Shaker Village

Suzanne MacDonald, shepherdess, Hancock Shaker Village

Thanks also to Roger Hall for information on the Shaker graveyard
in Harvard, Massachusetts; Robert P. Emlen for information on
George Kendall's map of Harvard; Scott Landis for information on
Shaker workbenches; and Martha Wetherbee for information
on Shaker baskets.

INDEX TO PHOTOGRAPHS

Shaker communities and museums welcome visitors. Those who wish to further identify the photographic sources in this book may refer to the page numbers given below.

Composed in Bodoni and Bodoni Book by
Trufont Typographers, Inc., Hicksville, New York.
Printed and bound by Toppan Printing Company, Ltd.,
Tokyo, Japan.